1

For my parents.

Preface

It was my dad who got me into boats, starting with a few fishing trips to Lake Arrowhead in Southern California. It was there, on the shores of a peaceful mountain lake in the middle of San Bernardino National Forest, he dropped an anchor on my foot. I was only five or six years old. My pinky toe still cranes off at an angle.

Later, when I was a little older, my dad took my brother and me fishing on the reservoirs and rivers in upstate New York. We fished with salmon eggs and all sorts of other baits now banned from the sport. He was patient and caring, reaching for the little jar of brine, taking out a salmon egg as if it were a magic bean, placing it carefully on a tiny gold colored hook at the end of my line. If I think about it hard enough, I can smell his tackle box. I can hear the quiet rumble of his old 5-1/2 horsepower Evinrude, smell its sweet blue-white exhaust.

He taught me how to cast, how to troll, and how to tie a knot. In my tackle box, I carry the last of his old bass lures and even some of his spinners. I never really use them. But they're with me. Sometimes, when I go fishing on a lake, which isn't too often these days, I take one of the old lures and fasten it to the end of my line. While my fishing buddy, John, motors us from one spot to another, I stare at the old lure and think about my dad, how he used to sit in the stern, one hand on the tiller of the Evinrude, the other holding his fishing rod. I remember how he used to stare at the rod tip and hold a bight of the line with his forefinger, ever so gentle.

In 1983 I left a good-paying job in professional fundraising to become a dive charter operator on the coast of Maine. I'm not sure my dad ever really understood what I was doing. While he respected and admired me, was incredibly proud of me, and loved me, he never said what he really felt . . . that he wanted me to be someone else, for my sake.

Few kids really get that, the feeling their father or mother truly respects them or admires them. I had that. It's a rare thing. My dad, I believe, felt the same way about my brother, now a surgical radiologist. How lucky were we to have a Dad who admired us for doing the things he felt he could not do himself?

And yet, I always knew he wanted me to be someone else. He never really accepted my leaving the city and that job.

My dad died in 1997. I wish I had told him how much I admired him, how much I respected him. How proud of him I was. I never found the time, or made the effort. Although, I believe, at the end, he knew how much I loved him.

During the last two hours of his life, I massaged his entire body. He was unable to speak at the time, dying of cancer, on morphine, but he touched my forearms and gazed into my eyes while I rubbed him down. I kept going like that as long as I could, praying my effort would drain him of life, ease his pain. I massaged him so he could die.

The end came about a half hour after I collapsed on the bed next to his. The hospice nurse woke me, said it was time, that he was taking his last few breaths. I got my brother and my mother; we gathered by his bedside.

The actual dying part was a mechanical thing. My dad, the part we loved, was gone before his body took its last breath.

There were no epiphanies. No revelations. Those would come later, in dribs and drabs. A conversation. A note from a friend of the family. An old photograph. An old letter.

It would be trite and an insult to his memory to say I hope he's fishing some quiet pond somewhere in the afterlife, pursuing the ever elusive quarry of his dreams. It's an insult because he was much bigger than that. He was bigger than the things he loved to do. . . . His was a selfless life . . . spent more for the benefit of others.

He never got the boat he always wanted, a 28' Bertram. He never got the cabin on the lake he always wanted in New England. He never got to see his oldest son achieve the greatness he envisioned for him.

But on his last night, during the final two hours of his life, I believe he realized everything would be just fine, if not exactly the way he had wanted it. He left this Earth as he lived his life, thinking of others. In fact, I believe the only thing he ever did just for himself was allow himself to die.

At the time, watching my father die was the hardest thing I ever had to do. Ten years later, my wife's youngest son, Daniel, died of a drug overdose at the age of twenty-one. In an instant the pain of watching my father die was trumped. I thought nothing could be worse than this poor kid's sad and untimely death and what it did to Sandra and her extended family.

Clearly, Daniel's loss, and in general, the loss of any child, is a parent's worst nightmare. Preface this with the long term suffering of a deteriorating disease and the experience of losing a child becomes even more painful and tragic.

In a sense, this is what a child goes through when a parent succumbs to Alzheimer's. It's the reverse -- a child's worst nightmare. With Alzheimer's, the parent becomes the child, and then something less, much, much less: a cruel amalgamation of child and adult, a vesicle of fear and doubt and confusion and sometimes terrible pain, with no future, no recourse and no ability to alter its destiny.

True, nothing in my life hurt as much as Daniel's loss. However, I think I can honestly say, of an equal rank was watching my mother die of Alzheimer's.

1. When My Father Died

This is a story about my mother. To tell it, I have to go back to 1994, when my father was first diagnosed with pancreatic cancer. Fortunately, for him, the symptoms of the disease manifested early. This is actually a good thing when it comes to cancer of the pancreas, because it gives a person options and a chance to go on the offensive. You have choices, surgery, chemo, and time to build up your mental fortitude. Some people who learn they have pancreatic cancer find out only after the disease has spread. These people usually get a few months. My father got three years and even managed to write a book while recovering from surgery and undergoing chemotherapy.

When my father first got sick it was pretty straight forward. He started peeing orange. The diagnosis came back in only a few days. Pancreatic cancer. We all went with him to the hospital to discuss what would happen next, survival rates, his treatment, etc. He decided on a course of moderate chemo and chose to get the Whipple operation, where they remove the pancreas, the gall bladder, a group of adjacent tissue containing lymph nodes and possibly a few other things. What they took out isn't really as important as what prompted my father's decision. He chose the Whipple because he wanted the tumor out and he figured surgery was a good shot at increasing his survival time. And he chose the less drastic chemo because he wanted to keep his hair. He was in his seventies and still had a good head of hair. Call it vain if you want. I call it pragmatic. He knew he was going to die anyway. Why not look good doing it?

That last sentiment might sound cavalier and even callous to some people reading this. I assure you, at the time, there was nothing cavalier about it. A decision had to be made, and my dad weighed his options and made his choice.

He took his last breath in his own bed on December 10, 1997, at about one in the morning, with me, my brother, my mother and a hospice nurse at his side. After he had passed, we all went our separate ways in the house. My brother went to his room. My mother went downstairs. And I went into the master bedroom with my dad's wallet. That wallet had a certain smell and a certain texture that I can remember as clearly as anything else I have ever know in my life. It's right up there with the smell of fresh cut grass and the taste of a snowflake on a cold winter's day.

In his master bedroom I held his wallet in my hands and sat on one of my mother's favorite chairs. I waited for the tears, but they didn't come. I tried to force them to come. I held the wallet to my face, smelled the soft leather, looked inside at all his credit cards, at the cards I'd seen him use dozens of times to buy me lunch or dinner or take us all on vacations. I wanted to cry but I just couldn't. I don't know why. Perhaps it's because he was a great man and he had lived a great life. He had accomplished so much and had achieved great success. And he had lived a fairly long time, to seventy-six years of age. I know that's not a record, or even, really, a satisfactory age for a modern, healthy American male. Most people would want more. My father wanted more. On his death bed he told me he had so much more he wanted to do.

Maybe I didn't cry that early December morning because I knew I had to be strong for my brother and mother. Already, a few days earlier, I had seen my brother collapse against a door casing and break down into sobs. And my mother. How was she handling it?

I sat there in her favorite chair for only a few minutes. When I realized I wasn't going to get emotional I put the wallet aside and went looking for my mother. I was solemn and quiet about it. I first looked in my brother's room. If I remember correctly he was in there talking to his wife on the phone, telling her what had happened and consoling her. I looked in my father's room, which used to be my room. He was in there, in my bed, what used to be my bed, the hospice nurse sitting sedately in the corner. I asked her if she knew where my mother was and she shook her head.

I walked downstairs and looked in the living room and the kitchen and the dining room. I didn't want to call for her. Whatever she was doing, whatever she was feeling, I didn't want to interfere in a jolting manner. Suffering through the loss of a loved one and having the shell of the person lying so near . . . it creates a certain atmosphere. Death requires respect, patience and obsequiousness.

Finally I went into the basement. We had a finished basement, a playroom, and off that was the laundry room. That's where I found her, in the laundry room. She was standing between the dryer and the ironing board folding my father's socks.

2. Taking Care of Mom

My father and I talked on an almost daily basis, until the day before he died. He was the same way with my brother. Kids, even as they enter adulthood, don't realize what it's like for a mom with two boys. Boy's don't have much patience for their moms. They call home and when their mom answers the first thing they say is: "Dad there?" In our house it got to the point where if we called and our father answered he would say, "Call back in ten minutes and I'll have your mother answer the phone. Talk to her." And he would hang up. He'd tell my mother the first call was a wrong number and then when we would call back ten minutes later he would deliberately not answer until she picked up or he would yell to her. "Judy, get the damn phone."

Her first words were always the same: "You want to talk to your father?" And we'd say no, we called to see how you were doing, at which time she would tell us about her day. Her garden. Her art work. The dinner she was cooking. Mundane stuff for impatient, insensitive boys to have to hear. I wonder if she knew we weren't giving her our full attention, and to this day, especially now, I wish to God I had taken the time in my life to really listen and appreciate her stories and special wisdom.

My father's fatal illness came on suddenly and progressed with the speed of a runaway locomotive. But he had a philosophy of life, both private and professional, that he summed up with the following phrase. "Never complain, never explain." What it means is that you don't saddle others with your problems, nor do you bother making excuses for mistakes you've made. He also believed a person shouldn't have to explain his or her actions to people after the fact, other than to say simply: I judged this to be the best course of action. Period. If you make a mistake, you learn from it, hopefully, make a correction and move on.

If you have to explain something you did, e.g. a speech you made, a comment or a direction you took, or explain something you created, a work of art for instance, then chances are the person who needs the explanation isn't getting it and never will, or the thing you did was lacking in clarity and/or purpose. Of course, there are exceptions, particularly when teaching children and others. But even here, in my experience the best teachers are the ones whose lessons speak for themselves.

My father never explained to us why a mother needed her son's affections and attention. He didn't have to. We knew what she needed by his actions: "Call back in ten minutes." Click!

And yet, we still didn't quite get it. Boys never do. But he must have known what he was doing, because he instilled in us a strong sense of responsibility.

3. Cancer Rears its Ugly Head

I was in Maine, living in a small house on the Saint George River, and working as the owner-operator of a 50' eco-tour boat. I was also writing magazine articles for a bunch of boating and fishing magazines. My brother was living in Indiana and working as an interventional radiologist in the greater Cincinnati area.

It was the summer of 1994. My mother and father came to visit. They took a room in a motel in Rockland and stayed at my house during the day. After my boat trips, which usually ran from 7:30 in the morning to 4:30 in the afternoon, I would drive home to meet up with them. We would have dinner together in my house or go out for a bite to eat. Sometimes we would just spend the day together, if I wasn't running the boat. Sometimes they would come out with me.

My father's illness first showed its ugly head at my house. I noticed how weak and unsteady he was on his feet. At one point, we took a walk down to the shore. I had to almost carry him down the hill. At another point, he almost broke his neck in my basement.

Talk about blind, stupid luck. That morning I knew they were coming over and I wanted to clean up a little. I went into the basement and vacuumed. While I was down there I moved an old upholstered chair out of my way. For some reason, the chair ended up at the bottom of the stairs, facing the very last step and about four feet away from it.

My house is small. One bedroom and a combination kitchen-living room-dining room. The stairs to the basement are in the middle of this big room and the stairwell is surrounded by a half-wall. There is no door from the main room of the house to the stairwell of the basement.

My mother and I were sitting on a couch that I had placed against the wall in the dining section of the main room when all of a sudden my father got up to walk around the open end of the basement stairwell. I think I asked him where he was going. He turned around to answer me and when he did he lost his footing and fell down the stairs backwards. I jumped up in an instant and headed for the stairs. I'm not sure if my mother screamed or called my dad's name or both. My mind was a blank. Pure response mode. Pure adrenaline.

What I expected to find was my father with a broken neck at the bottom of the stairs. Instead I found him sitting in the upholstered chair I had moved earlier in the day. Apparently, he had fallen in such a way that he was able to take four steps at a time, backwards, until he finally lost his footing, tripped on the last step and landed squarely in the chair. He didn't have a scratch or a bump on him. On the other hand, my mother and I needed a defibrillator.

About an hour or two later, my father went to the bathroom. I heard him call out to my mother. "Judy, come here a minute. I'm pissing orange. What is this?"

She went into to see what he wanted and I heard her say: "It's bile Irving, or blood. You have to see a doctor."

And that, as they say, was that. They left for home the next day and my father got in to see his doctor that week. Diagnosis: Pancreatic cancer. Prognosis: Not good. It never is with pancreatic cancer.

In the early eighties my father had a heart attack. He gave up everything to get better, went on a regimen of medicines and exercise. My mom, bless her heart, turned his life around with a vitamin rich, fat free diet and a completely fresh attitude toward eating and living. She became a heart-healthy advocate and read everything she could about the subject. She learned how to be a holistic-oriented provider and spent every waking hour working to heal and protect him. She did such a good job that when he ended up in Intensive Care for three weeks after his Whipple surgery his doctors could find no evidence of heart damage. At one point, near death, his kidneys were on the verge of shutting down, and his heart was beating at over 190 beats per minute -- for 48 hours straight! The on-call cardiologist came up to me and asked if I was absolutely sure my father had ever had a heart attack. He said a person who had had a heart attack would not normally survive this type of stress, and he was convinced my father had been misdiagnosed. I assured him that my father had indeed suffered a heart attack and that he had been treated by a top notch team of doctors at Beth Israel Hospital in New York. The on-call cardiologist wasn't convinced.

What he didn't know, couldn't have known, was that my mother's determination and dedication to curing and healing my father's heart had seen no bounds. She had never considered for even one-second that that she couldn't succeed in fixing him.

But cancer of the pancreas? This, my mother knew, was something she could not fix.

4. Secrets

It was my uncle who called me from my parents' house in New York to tell me my father had fallen in the shower and couldn't get up. Why didn't my mother call? That's a good question. I don't know, and I never will. It wasn't the first time she failed to inform my brother or me about something important, or tried to keep something a secret, if that was her intent.

For years growing up we had been told my real grandfather on my mother's side had died of an aneurism at the age of thirty-nine. In fact, even my mother's younger sisters and my cousins believed the story. One day, when I was in my thirties, my mother let it slip that he had been murdered by a jealous spouse, hit over the head with a steel pipe. She said her father was a notorious philanderer, that they had owned a hardware/general store in Mayaguez, Puerto Rico and that he had been fooling around with the wives of some of his patrons.

My mother also kept my dad's heart attack a secret, or tried to. They had gone to Israel on a business trip. My dad had a speaking engagement and during the event he had chest pain. He ended up in the hospital. The Israeli doctors told him he had had a heart attack and that he probably needed surgery but that he was safe to return home as long as he didn't strain himself. So they both boarded a plane and flew back to New York. They landed at Kennedy International Airport and went straight to the family physician. He took some tests and when the results came back he sent my father right over to Beth Israel Hospital.

That was when my mother should have called us. But she didn't. In fact, I only found out about his condition through his office. I drove straight down and met them both at the hospital and I gave my mother hell for not calling. She did not really explain herself.

Never complain, never explain.

The third and final time I learned of a secret she had kept to herself was the night we found out my father wasn't coming out of the ICU. It was the night we realized the doctors had screwed-up and placed his life in serious jeopardy.[1]

We were driving back to the house in my father's car. I was at the wheel, my mother in the passenger seat, and my brother in the back. My mother teared-up and said, "He'll never forgive me, never. I should have told him."

She began to sob and repeat herself, "He'll never forgive me. I should have told him."

We had no idea what she was talking about, and we tried to console her. We told her everything would be all right. He was a tough son of a gun. He would pull through this.

Finally, after a bit of back and forth, it came out.

We had a little dog named Chickie. She was a miniature Schnauzer. My father loved the dog. It was all part of the WWII vets American dream. The house, the wife, the two

---

[1]My father had dehydrated because the night before his surgery nobody had started an IV fluid drip. The actual surgery the following morning went very quickly, too quickly, so there had been very little fluid replacement in the operating room. By the time he got to the ICU his kidneys were on the verge of shutting down. From this point on the doctors were playing a game of catch-up.

kids, the two cars and the dog. But one day the dog ran away and never came back, or so we thought.

That night, while driving back to the house with my mother sobbing next to me and my brother in the back seat, we learned the truth about Chickie.

She had given it away.

My brother and I have two distinctly different recollections as to why she gave the dog away. One recollection is considerably less admirable than the other. I believe my memory is accurate and that my brother's is colored by issues relating to the incredible stress he was under at the time.[2] But to be fair, I'm going to give both recollections.

I believe my mother gave the dog away because of my father's allergies. He had terrible allergies, which made him a slave to pharmaceuticals. Inhalers, sinus sprays, antihistamines, antibiotics, anti-inflammatory medicines. He even underwent painful surgeries on a routine basis to remove nasal polyps. My mother hated to see him suffer,

---

[2] I love my brother dearly, but he didn't work with my father, nor did he travel with him on business. That "grooming" privilege was given to me, rightly or wrongly, as the older sibling. My father worked with attractive women. He had a personal secretarial pool of four and got phone calls, weekends and nights, from his administrative assistant. He worked for years with the Hollywood elite as a fundraiser in Los Angeles. Jealousy was there, but it was always kept in check. Furthermore, at the time of the surgery, my brother was dealing with dad's doctors, his own very difficult work situation and a serious health issue with one of his kids. I can't blame him for transposing one memory onto another.

and she knew deep in her heart that the dog was not helping the situation and almost certainly was partly to blame. But my dad would never get rid of the dog. Never in a million years. So she told him it had run away.

My brother remembers it thus: She gave the dog away because she was jealous. She hated it when my father would come home from work and say hello and kiss the dog before saying hello and kissing her.

Actually, he's not wrong about this happening or about her being jealous. It did happen and she was upset about the attention he gave to the dog. But he's confusing the two memories. She did indeed have a problem with my father coming home and saying hello and playing with the dog first, but she confronted him about it and told him specifically that he was not to do it anymore. It was pretty much of an ultimatum and he complied.

Either way, it's not the why that's important but the fact that my mother, for whatever reason, could keep a secret. Also, for whatever reason, she did not call me when my father had his heart attack.[3] Nor did she call me when he fell in the shower. She called my Uncle, and it was my Uncle who called me.

"Robby." He always called me Robby. "You better get down here. He fell in the shower and your mother couldn't get him up."

I was seven and a half hours up the coast in my little house on the river. I packed a bag and the dog and headed to New

---

[3] I'm not a psychologist or a shrink but it is possible her issue here has its roots in her father's murder. Or as it can happen to many of us, she was in denial.

York. I knew I was driving down to take care of my dad in his final few days on this Earth.

He lasted eight.

5. It Starts

I remained in New York for an additional three weeks after my father's funeral. Any kid who has dealt with the death of the family's breadwinner/provider knows what I'm talking about. I was fortunate in that my mother had a fairly good handle on the day to day operations of the house. In the forty-six years of their marriage my mother always took care of the house and kids, while my father focused on an incredibly demanding career as a professional fundraiser, for which he travelled extensively and worked all hours of the day and night.

It was my mom who hired and fired lawn and garden workers, landscapers, roofing contractors, stone masons, carpenters, plumbers, electricians, the occasional housekeeper and all manner of suburban laborers and other service people. She made our lunches for school, drove us to and from basketball and karate practice, organized birthdays and holidays, took care of my father's father (who lived with us for a time before he himself got sick and died of pancreatic cancer), found time to volunteer at a nursing home, planted and tended non-indigenous fruit trees and other exotic species in her garden and even studied art and became an accomplished painter and sculptor.

But she didn't pay the bills. My father did that.

To make things easier on her I got a power of attorney and established a means by which I could take over the monthly chores of bill paying. All she had to do was put all the bills in a basket in my dad's old office and I would come home the third week of every month and take care of them. If anything needed to be done around the house I would take care of that, too.

This is how it began.

Coincidentally, I was in New York with my mother when the ice storm of 1998 hit on January 4. Where I live and had my boat berthed at the time, the midcoast area of Maine (the house in St. George, the boat in Rockland), the damage wasn't too bad. The worst of the storm had hit upstate New York, Ontario, the northwest tip of Vermont, and parts of Maine to the north and east of Rockland. I was lucky. In north Yonkers, where my parents house was, we just had rain.

A friend back in Maine looked in on my boat, a 50' wooden eco-tour boat licensed for 49 passengers, and according to him everything I owned and worried about, including my house and yard, had weathered the storm. But the event was a harsh reminder that I had a life and job to which I had to return. I hated to do it, to leave my mom in the house that her husband had died in, to leave her in her grief and uncertainty, but she assured me she would be all right. Her friends, her rabbi, her fellow congregants at her synagogue, the other volunteers and staff at the nursing home, and her Japanese garden club group, would help her in the months ahead. Her sister in the Bronx and her best friend, Anna, who had lost her husband a few years prior and who lived only a couple of miles away, would also be of great help.

One time, when I was a little kid, my mother took me to visit a friend of hers in the neighborhood. While she and her friend and a couple of other neighborhood Moms were having tea inside, I went out to watch her son practice fly casting at the edge of their swimming pool. Suddenly, I felt a tugging in my eye. The idiot had hooked me in the eyelid and part of my eye. He started reeling in. I yelled. He yelled. My mother and her friends appeared, and everyone but my mother was freaking out. She looked at me, bit through the fishing line, then calmly took me by the arm into the house. She led me into the bathroom and sat me down on the toilet under the bright light. With a gentle and knowing touch and a flashlight she removed the hook from my eye.

Did I really need to worry about this woman?

6. Strange Behavior

There were signs of my mother's illness very early on that I never noticed. For that matter, nobody else noticed, either. Or if they noticed, they didn't attribute it to Alzheimer's or dementia. I can remember one time a few years before his death, my father had gotten into a fight with my mother about something and I called him out on it. I said he was being too hard on her. He told me I didn't understand but that I would in due time. His words were something to the effect: "Your mother can be difficult at times. Just wait. You'll see."

He had other special phrases for my mother, too. These he used endearingly. He would say, "Your mother's an f'n genius." And, "Your mother can be frugal to a fault."[4]

Dad's words would turn out to be more prophetic than either one of us could have imagined. How could he have known that he would die before she did? How did he know I would end up being her primary care giver?

In any case, the very first inklings of trouble came the day I packed up my gear and the dog and prepared to head back for Maine. The previous night I told her I was leaving and asked if she needed anything before I left. She said she was in good shape. I asked if she needed anything more done around the house. She said she didn't.

But that morning, as I got in the truck and turned the key to the ignition, she asked me to come back inside and help her with something. I was furious. I wanted to beat the traffic and be home before dark. But I complied. I shut off the

---

[4] In her words, she would say: "I know how to polish a dime."

engine and went back inside. One thing led to another, one more little thing to do piled on top of another. I became impatient and eventually lost my temper. "Why didn't you think of these things last night, or two days ago?" I asked. "I told you I had to go and that I wanted to beat the traffic, I have an eight hour drive!"

She yelled at me. I yelled at her. We fought like a pair of banshees. I did what she wanted me to do and then I left in a huff. Forty minutes later, while on Route 684 heading onto I-84 in Connecticut, I felt so bad I had to call her. I'm not sure I apologized (apologies are not usually in my repertoire) but I asked her if she was OK and told I would be back in two weeks. I told her to make a list and I would take care of everything when I got back. Before I hung up I told her I loved her. "I love you too," she said. "Drive safe."

And herein lies a perfect example of how stupid sons can be, or at least this son. For months after my father's death, every time I prepared to leave my mom and head back to Maine, she would do the same thing. She would come up with a dozen last minute jobs for me to do. She knew I was in a hurry. She knew I was impatient to leave and beat the traffic. None of that mattered. As I stepped into the truck, she'd ask me to do something. And every time she did this we would get into a yelling match. The scenario played itself out repeatedly, visit after visit, for months, until I figured out what was going on.

She didn't want me to leave.

Like I said, stupid. Stupid. Stupid. Stupid.

Finally, I used a different approach. Instead of getting impatient and yelling at her, I gave her a big hug and told her I loved her. She laughed, and said she loved me. And we hugged. And then I got in the truck and left.

It was that simple.

Sons. Boys. Men. We just don't really think of this stuff.

But here's the point of this anecdote. My mother's behavior was not really normal for her. It was out of character. It was almost as if she had momentarily reverted to being a little girl. The mother I knew didn't mince words or play manipulative mind games. If she had something on her mind she would just spill it. And yet here she was, acting out in an unfiltered, unrestrained, knee jerk fashion. Did it occur to me at the time this was a sign of Alzheimer's or dementia? Of course not.

The sad truth is that Alzheimer's hits people long before it's ever diagnosed. Friends, family, even your doctors, won't start considering dementia or Alzheimer's until it has become painfully obvious, usually as the result of a memory issue. The person becomes repetitive or continually forgets appointments. They mistake the washer for the dryer or forget where the ignition key goes in the car. But the earliest signs of dementia and Alzheimer's are not related to memory. They are behavioral.

Just a few months after my dad's death, my mother started going through doctors like most people go through groceries. You would think one of her doctors, e.g. her cardiologist, eye doctor, dentist, internist, etc., would have asked her for the name and number of a contact person or somebody in the family they could talk to about her health and welfare. You would think that one of these professional medical people would have had the presence of mind to see the early signs of Alzheimer's and make it known to someone close to the patient. Well, all I can say about this is that my mother either had the worst doctors in the Greater New York area, or they just didn't care, or dementia and Alzheimer's is very difficult to identify in its earliest form.

This one doctor, a cardiologist who had been treating my mother's labial high blood pressure for years and who had an office in White Plains, N.Y., sent her from the office crying. She phoned in tears to tell me the doctor had called her a stupid woman. Shame on me for not going to the guy's office and personally showing him a technique whereby he can perform a colonoscopy with his own stethoscope.

Why would a doctor say something so cruel and insensitive? Because he was too self-absorbed and self-important to register the early signs of Alzheimer's in one of his own patients. If a patient's own doctors can't see the early signs of dementia and Alzheimer's how will anyone else?

My mother stopped seeing this doctor, for obvious reasons, and started seeing one who had been recommended by her best friend Anna. Anna also recommended an eye doctor, who would later perform unnecessary cataract surgery on my mother and cause her to lose almost all the vision in one of her eyes.

7. Doctors and Diet

While the behavioral clues mentioned earlier hint at dementia and/or Alzheimer's, another clue that the disease might be poking its ugly head out of the shell is a person's gastrointestinal health. If the person is still living on their own and taking care of themselves and you look in the refrigerator and see food that has obviously gone by its expiration date, or you check the silverware drawer and the cupboards and see that utensils, plates, bowls and cups have been put away unclean, there's a chance something is not quite right.

My mother had it in her head she had a serious gastrointestinal problem. She scheduled a colonoscopy and an upper GI Series. I drove down to New York and took her in to Miseracordia Hospital Medical Center in the Bronx. Her doctor was in his eighties and was scheduled to retire a few days later. The procedure he performed on my mother was to be just about the last one of his career. This turned out to be a major pain in the ass, figuratively and literally, because when my mother needed some follow-up information, none was available. The old coot left the hospital and never looked back, his office closed, and nobody in the department picked up his patient load.

Fortunately, according to the doctor's report, my mother was fine. She had a little diverticulitis, which is normal for a person her age, but no polyps and nothing that would cause her gastrointestinal difficulty.

However, she didn't believe any of this, and she wanted to talk to the doctor to schedule more tests. That's how I found out about his retirement. It didn't make her very happy to hear the guy had disappeared from the face of the Earth like a wanted member of the Gambino crime family but eventually we were able to put that behind us, because this is about the time I noticed the spoiled food in the refrigerator and the dirty dishes and silverware in the drawers and cupboards.

The first thing I did was throw out the old food and wash the dishes. It made my mom furious that I would waste food and redo what she had already done. "What are you doing? There's nothing wrong with the food. It's in the refrigerator. What's the point of having a refrigerator if it can't keep food from spoiling?"

So I bought a new refrigerator and took the old one home to my house later in the week.

I also tried to explain about expiration dates and using enough soap. She wasn't hearing or listening. To her, if it's in the refrigerator and it's cold, it's forever. If the food went bad it must be because the refrigerator is broken. And there no reason to use a lot of soap. Soap's just a marketing gimmick. They want you to use more concentrated soap than you need. My mother used to dilute her soap. Over time, the dilution kept getting weaker and weaker, until it was almost nothing but plain water. Before long she would just be rinsing her dishes under hot water.

And then came the second revelation: The amount of ice cream she was eating. The freezer was full of old cartons of half-eaten ice cream. I would say to her: "Mom, aren't you lactose intolerant? Should you be eating ice cream?"

And yet, Alzheimer's never entered into the equation or discussion. As far as I was concerned my mother was just a quirky, difficult, stubborn old lady who liked to do things her way.

Incidentally, these interactions were never pleasant. They often involved raised voices and usually ended in tears. Hers.

8. Just Getting Old

My father had been dead for a few months, and I had been commuting to and from New York about every two weeks. When I think back on that time I realize now it was the start of a drastic lifestyle change that would completely encompass the next fifteen years of my life. My father passed away in 1997. Before he died he told me, "Your mother can be difficult." After he died I came to realize just how right he was. But my mother wasn't officially diagnosed with Alzheimer's until 2004, a year after I had moved her out of her home of forty years and into the Maine house my wife and I were living in.

She would live with us for about six months and eventually move into a house that was built for her next to ours. She would live in the new house for three years before going into residential care.

In 1998 and 1999, we were all still terribly naive and stupid and didn't have a clue that my mother was suffering the earliest stages of dementia and Alzheimer's. Would it have made a difference had we known? Absolutely! I doubt we would have built the house for her had we known she would need special care three years down the road.

All the above didn't much matter, because back then Alzheimer's never came up in conversation, not with my brother, my mother's sister, my mother's doctors or her friends. And I was still dealing with the day to day problems of my mother's physical health and her doctor's visits and the house maintenance problems and her financial situation and a few other wrinkles that began to pop up, and never once did I say to myself, "Wait a minute. Is something else going on here other than old age?"

There was the time one summer I got down to the house in New York in the middle of a heat wave. My mother was seated at the kitchen table with the windows closed, the fans off and the air conditioner broken. She was on the verge of heat prostration. I asked her why she didn't call me about the broken air conditioner and she said she didn't need it. She wasn't hot. Meanwhile, sweat poured off her forehead in streams, and her clothes were drenched. I immediately got her into a cool shower and called the HVAC people. Even they couldn't believe how hot it was in the house. It must have been 115 degrees.

On another visit, while going through some mail and papers on the desk, I came across a signed loan agreement for a car. The car was in some guy's name, a name I had never heard before, and my mother's signature was in the cosigner's box. I asked her if she was buying a car for someone and she said that she met a guy who was doing some work for her and he needed a car. Apparently, the guy had gone to the bank and taken out an auto loan form and brought it to her and persuaded her to sign it. It took me awhile to find out where he worked but when I did I stopped in to see him and we had a nice chat. He decided not to come around the house anymore.

One Thanksgiving (actually it was a few days afterwards) my mother and I were having a talk in the kitchen. I asked her what she did for the holiday and she said she drove down to my cousins in Mt. Vernon and had a lovely Thanksgiving dinner with him, his wife, my mother's sister and a few of their friends. She said she had a wonderful time except she got lost coming home and a police officer yelled at her. I asked her what had happened and she said that somewhere around the Bronx River Parkway she saw a lot of police cars and blue lights flashing and decided to ask for directions. Apparently the cop hollered something to the effect: "Lady! Get the hell out of here! Can't you see we're in the middle of a serious situation?"

I can just picture my mother walking through a hail of gunfire between twenty cops and a dozen bank robbers and asking a nice policeman if he can direct her to the Garth Road exit.

Absolute truth, but she said she didn't just drive off and take no for an answer. She scolded the cop for being rude and pressed him further for the directions.

Finally, according to her, the cop threatened to arrest her if she didn't leave.

"Can you believe the nerve of the man," she said to me. "I don't care how busy he was, he should have helped me with directions."

I just shook my head. My mother had become Granny Magoo.

9. Bad Decisions Cause Physical Problems

There were a few things that happened in fairly quick succession, each one about two weeks apart, which, when considered alone, might have been inconsequential to some people and, perhaps for others, attributed to bad luck. But each one, when taken as part of a sequence of events, signaled the turning point for both our lives and prompted the decision for her to leave the old house in New York and move in with me and my wife.

The first of these occurrences was a fall she took at her synagogue. She always drove herself to synagogue every Saturday. She used to go on Fridays, too, but knew better than to drive at night. So unless one of her friends took her to Friday night services she satisfied herself with Saturdays and Holidays.

One Saturday, while she was in the outer sanctum talking to some people, she decided to show them her exercise routine. Dressed to the nines, wearing a pair of three or four inch heels, she showed them what she does every morning when she gets up and every night before she goes to bed. One arm up. Opposite leg up. Then the other arm up and the other, opposing leg up. Like a stork. She used to do this all the time. Only this time, standing on the slick, recently waxed tile floor, in her high heels, she slipped and fell and hurt her back.

I was in Maine at the time and didn't find out about this for quite awhile. It was a month or two before her good friend from synagogue (I'll call him Dr. M.) told me what had happened.[5]

---

[5] Dr. M, a widower for many years, started spending more time with my mom after my father died. He had romantic

34

From this day forward, my mother blamed everything that bothered her, her back, her wrists, her arthritis, her bowels, her stomach, her eyesight, you name it, on this fall. It became a common refrain. "My stomach hasn't been the same since The Fall."

The Fall. In Capital Letters.

On my next visit to New York I happened to stop in at my neighbor's across the street. It was always a pleasant diversion to say hello to Mrs. S. and check in on her husband, who had been very sick and bed ridden for years. While we were catching up she told me that my mother had gotten into a pushing match with the neighbor adjacent to her.

I was shocked. I knew she had some issues with her neighbors because she was complaining to me about them, e.g. this one had too many cats. That one's trees were ruining her rock wall. The other one was encroaching her property line with plantings. But to get into a physical altercation. That wasn't her.

A couple of weeks later I got a call from Dr. M., who was with my mother at the hospital. "She's OK," he said. "Turns out she was just dehydrated."

I left my house in Maine immediately and made it to the hospital in about eight hours. They had her on IV fluids,

---

interests, but they took a back seat to his simply being there and caring for my mother. I was lucky to have him as a thoughtful and attentive companion to my mother. After the fall, he took her to the hospital and had her checked out. X-rays. CAT scans. Whatever she needed.

and she was responding well. The attending doctor told me she was sure my mother was simply dehydrated but thought it best to keep her overnight. I thanked Dr. M., who told me he found her slumped over the kitchen table. When I went in to see her, she blamed it on The Fall.

I brought her home the next day and then spent a few days with her. I did some shopping, took care of the bills and fixed a few things at the house. The day I was to leave to go back to Maine, I was sitting at the kitchen table watching her get some lunch together. She tried to get into the silverware drawer. It got jammed. She struggled, and before I could get out of my chair to help her she cursed, yanked the whole drawer out of the aperture, and dumped the entire contents of knives, forks, spoons and other utensils on the floor. The she yelled:

"I HATE THIS HOUSE!"

That was the moment for me. That was the moment I knew it was time for her to leave. My father had died in his own bed, in his own house, on his own terms. My mother would not be so lucky. I would take her from the house, build another house for her, and before all was said and done, she would lose control of her destiny.

10. Promises to Break

On one of my many visits to see her in New York I came home after visiting friends to find her at the kitchen table crying her eyes out. She was, for all practical purposes, in a frantic state. I also saw that she was polishing a piece of jewelry. I came up to her and hugged her and asked her what was wrong. With tears in her eyes, and her voice cracking, she told me the following:

"I was in the nursing home visiting with one of the residents. This woman is very sick. She can't talk and she's bedridden. She had silver earrings in her ears that were green with tarnish. I asked her if she wanted me to clean them and I thought she said yes so I took them out of her ears and brought them home to clean."

"That's great, Ma," I said. "She'll love that."

The tears flowed freely.

"But I can't find it," she said.

"What? What can't you find?"

"I can't find one of the earrings. I can't find it anywhere. I put it down somewhere and I can't find it."

I'm sure she had been sitting in the chair at the kitchen table cleaning that one earring for hours, probably crying the whole time, agonizing over the earring she couldn't find.

"We'll find it, Ma. I'm sure it's here. Maybe it's upstairs by your bed."

We found it eventually. And it was a God send. But that night my mother called me into her room and made me promise I would never, ever put her in a nursing home.

"No, Ma. You'll never have to do anything you don't want to do."

"Promise me."

"I promise, Ma. You'll never to be in a nursing home."

11. Physically, It Gets More Serious

The last thing that went sour for my mother in New York was her eye surgery. I mentioned she had been going through doctors like most people go through their underwear. Well, she decided she needed a new eye doctor. She talked to her friend Anna about it and Anna suggested she go to the eye surgeon who had done Anna's eyes. Little did Anna or my mother realize, they were talking about two different things. Anna had gotten radial keratotomy, not cataract surgery. Anyway, Anna took my mother to see her own doctor and before I knew what was going on I was on my way down to New York again.

By the time I got down there she had already had one eye done. I drove her in for a follow up visit because she was complaining of discomfort and vision problems.

The office was an eye surgery factory that didn't inspire a great deal of confidence. I wish I would have just talked her out of having the second eye done there but I let her go through the second surgery, which ended badly.

In an effort to cut down on post procedure discomfort, the doctor put a patch on her eye and told her to keep it on for a full 48 hours. I stayed with her in New York to make sure she complied and then took her back to the doctor's office for her follow-up.

There I was, waiting in the crowded outer reception area when I heard my mom screaming in pain. I rushed into one of the recovery rooms to find her holding her eye and yelling: "It hurts. It hurts."

She was sitting in a chair in the center of a room that was lit up like the surface of the sun. An aide or a nurse or the guy who emptied the garbage cans and cleaned the floors had just taken her patch off and was looking at me without a clue as to what was happening.

"What's going on?" I said.

"I don't know," he said. " I took the patch off and she started screaming. I can't get her to tell me anything."

"Where's the doctor?"

"He's out to lunch."

"Well get him back here."

The idiot left to call the doctor and I looked around the room. I was wondering why an eye specialist would use a room that was lit up like the surface of the sun to take off a patch that had been on someone's eye for 48 hours.

Turns out my mom suffered an eschemia of some kind in her eye when this nurse's aid took off her patch. In other words, she had a little stroke in her eye. That, or she hemorrhaged, or threw a small blood clot. Whatever, the stress the eye was under having gone from pitch black for 48 hours to super bright light, literally, in the blink of an eye, was too much for her. It would have been too much for anyone who had labile hypertension and who was on blood pressure medications.

This doctor had never checked with my mother's cardiologist, who, it so happened, was a new one, given that her previous doctor had called her, "a stupid woman." Had the eye doctor checked, he would have realized my mother was going through some adjustments to new drugs.

I'm still at a loss to understand why an eye doctor's office would have a room full of bright lights for removing patches or dealing with dilated eyes.

To make things worse, I found out from my mother's former ophthalmologist that she didn't have cataracts. She didn't need surgery. All she needed was a new pair of glasses.

The bottom line is: she ended-up losing most of her vision in the eye.

Maybe one can attribute these things, The Fall, The Dehydration, The Pushing Match, The Tantrum at the Silverware Drawer, The botched Eye Surgery, as a consequence to getting old. Not so. Each of these things are a cause and effect type of occurrence. They all relate to a lack of judgement or a clear way of thinking things through.

The Fall happened because my mom had started to repeat things over and over again. As the disease evolved and her mental capacity shrank, so did her ability to communicate ideas and experiences other than the ones she most focused on or about which she was most obsessed. These were the things she did routinely her whole life, in this case, her exercises. She would tell everyone and want to demonstrate how she would balance on one leg.

The Dehydration. She simply forgot to drink water and keep herself cool.

The Pushing Match. A very common behavioral development in the early stages of Alzheimer's. Basically it comes down to this: I am right, everybody else is wrong.

The Silverware Drawer got stuck because my mother kept stuffing things into it. She kept stuffing things into because she couldn't throw anything away. She couldn't throw anything away because she was afraid to be without a given utensil. If she needed a potato peeler and couldn't find one, she would buy another one at the store. She probably had three or four potato peelers in the drawer.

Lastly, the eye surgery. She thought she was getting a radial keratotomy, same thing Anna got. She wasn't. She was getting cataract surgery she didn't need.

12. They Say They Know But They Don't

When people hear you say your mother or father has Alzheimer's you often get a response something on the order of, "Oh, I'm so sorry. I know how awful it is. My grandfather (or grandmother, uncle, etc.) had it."

The sentiment and sympathy is appreciated, for sure. Unfortunately, I don't believe a lot of the people who respond this way really understand the deep, insidious nature of the disease. For the most part, they think people who suffer from Alzheimer's forget things or wander off on their own and get lost. Spending limited time with someone who has (or had) severe dementia, Alzheimer's or another type of deteriorating brain condition, being with them once in a while, on holidays or a few times every month, can't possibly give an observer a complete picture.

There are only two types of people who know what it's like: family members who live with and/or care for someone who has the disease, and health care specialists who deal with it professionally on a daily basis.

I'm not trying to be callous or snide. I'm speaking from my own experience, as someone who said these things to people who were going through what I finally went through myself. I even used to tell a joke about it:

Q: "What's the great thing about Alzheimer's?"

A: "All the new people you meet."

I used to think that was funny.

Indeed, Alzheimer's can be very funny. It's funny, cruel, sad, painful, frustrating, spiritually eviscerating, all at the same time. And there's a helplessness and hopelessness to it, more so than most anyone can imagine. Believe me, my mother said and did things that would have been hysterical if they hadn't been so penetratingly sad at their core. Like the time she drove with me to take a load of trash and recyclables to the dump. As we pulled through the gate of the facility, she turned to me and said: "Oh, yes, you took me to eat here once."

I had a friend many years ago whose father suffered from the disease. One evening my friend asked me if I would like to have dinner with him, his wife and his father. I agreed. "Just so you know," he said, "my father has Alzheimer's."

"That's OK," I told him. "It's no problem for me."

At the restaurant, his father ordered an orange juice and when it arrived he yelled at the waitress for bringing milk. My friend just said: "No, Dad. It is orange juice. It's OK." And my friend apologized to the waitress. He was very patient and kind with his father but there was something in his voice I didn't quite recognize or think about until years later, when my own situation began to mimic his.

For years and years, until my mother began to exhibit symptoms of the disease, this is what I knew of Alzheimer's: the embarrassment of mistaking orange juice for milk . . . losing your memories, forgetting loved ones, not remembering how to start your car or do your laundry. If only this were the worst of it.

To truly appreciate the cruelty imposed by the disease you have to witness the slow degradation of mental capacity in a loved one over a period of years. And to really grasp the horror of end stage Alzheimer's one has be with the person when they become incapacitated by uncontrollable and painful spasms, or be there when they can no longer chew their food, swallow, or hold the weight of their head in an upright position on their own shoulders.

What was the something I heard in my friend's voice that day at the restaurant? It was the sound of total submission or resignation.

I've spent time with loved ones and close friends who have died from other deadly maladies. Even with a death sentence hanging over their heads, e.g., cancer, arteriosclerosis, emphysema, etc., they continue to live their lives. They fight the disease, whether it's chemotherapy, surgery, radiation, and carry on for as long as they can, or as long as they choose. Some may choose to live out their lives as best as they can without the procedural trappings of modern medicine. Some may have more time than others, and some may get caught unprepared and in a coma. However, for the most part, people who face death with their mental capacity intact, have the opportunity to make their plans, say their goodbyes and enter into a state of acceptance.

People with Alzheimer's, dementia and other forms of severe mental dysfunction, as well as their caregivers, don't usually get this opportunity. There always seems to be a tomorrow. Perhaps this is because these types of diseases have no definitive prognosis, i.e., they affect everyone differently. Moreover, they can go on for as long as a dozen or more years, maybe as long as twenty years. They'll fool you into thinking there's time enough to plan and say your goodbyes. But . . . before you know what's happening, there's no time to plan, no chance for alternatives, no way to control what comes next.

And before you know it, it's too late for goodbyes.

For me, at this time, late in the year 2000. I wasn't beaten. I hadn't submitted. I didn't even realize my mother had Alzheimer's.

13. Change Equals Stress

As further proof the time had come for her to leave New York, my mother's rabbi called to tell me she was having a rough time in synagogue, her last place of spiritual and social refuge. I contacted her friends Dr. M. and Anna, and her sister in the Bronx, and told them I was thinking about selling the house and moving her up to live with us in Maine. Although they weren't happy about her leaving for someplace so far away, they all agreed it was time for her to find more suitable living arrangements. In their minds, and mine, the house had just gotten to be too much for her.

It wasn't quite as drastic a change of venue as it sounds. We had managed a few dry runs over the previous months. I would come down on one of my biweekly visits, but instead of leaving her at the house in New York and heading back on my own, I would pack a bag with her clothes and take her with me. She would live with us for a few weeks and then I'd bring her back to New York for a couple of weeks. Back and forth. Back and forth. It sounds exhausting but it was actually easier to have her with us. I even brought her sister with us one time. And my mother seemed to genuinely like living with us in Maine. She joined the local synagogue and the garden club and spent quality time with my wife, Sandra, and her mom. She also started meeting some of our neighbors and their extended families.

On one of these stays in Maine we noticed a lot for sale a few hundred yards from where we lived. I asked my mother if she was ready to leave her house in New York and move to Maine and she was 100% behind the idea. We bought a book of house plans and started thumbing through various types of homes. I remember her saying: "I want a house with a lot of natural light. The house in New York is very dark."

It was. It was a colonial built in 1936. Small rooms. Small windows.

The house we eventually picked for Maine was a modified cape with master and guest bedrooms and a laundry room on the first floor. I made sure it had many windows and a couple of skylights for natural light. Curiously, after she moved in, which wouldn't happen until February 2003, she would keep the blinds closed day and night. Her bright, airy house, with lots of windows and skylights, was always darker than the inside of a pocket.

And so began one of the biggest changes of my mother's life. The move to Maine. I wondered how she would handle it.

Back in 1967 a couple of psychiatrists at a medical school devised a stress test based on a list of the most emotionally taxing things that can happen in a person's life. Tops on the list was the death of a spouse, then divorce, then marital separation, then jail term, and then death of a close family member. Those are the top five. There are another thirty-eight events on the list, not all of them bad.

Strangely enough, moving out of your house of forty years isn't on the list.[6]

---

[6] The list was developed by Thomas Holmes and Richard Rahe, two psychiatrists, at the University of Washington School of Medicine, after studying the medical records of over 5,000 patients.

14. Moving to Maine

I secured a real estate agent for the house in New York and a builder for the Maine home, talked to the bank, interviewed movers and started prepping the old house for visitors. I made it clear to the real estate agent that no one would be allowed to view the house without being accompanied by her or another qualified member of her staff. She knew the situation with my mom, and I felt I could trust her.

Before the house sold everything inside had to be packed and sorted. My father had an antique and antiquities collection that needed to be handled with special care, and forty years worth of accumulated stuff, which had never once been culled, had to be sorted and packed. They saved everything. Everything! And I had to figure out what to move on my own and what to leave for the professionals to move.

A friend and I spent three days packing the books. I spent another three weeks packing the valuables. Two more solid weeks were spent packing with Sandra. I personally rented three, large U-haul trucks on three different occasions. In addition, the movers spent a week packing up the rooms and filling an entire semi-truck and trailer. The books and antiques went to the basement of my house and Sandra's house. Everything else was going to have to go into temporary storage.

The good thing about this whole process was that it helped my mom focus. She got into packing and labeling things and the job kept her busy, and, dare I say, out of trouble for a couple of months. Unfortunately, it opened up a Pandora's box of other issues.

We started some of the packing before the house found a buyer, but the bulk of it had to be done after we were under contract. Moreover, I ended-up filling the third U-haul truck and a utility trailer the day of the closing.

The last three days of the move were among the most stressful days I've ever experienced. The house had to be completely empty by the time of the closing. So, here we were, me and Sandra, taking stuff to the curb to be picked-up by the garbage collectors, and my mother, sneaking down to the curb afterwards and grabbing the stuff we had just thrown out in order to hand it to one of the movers in the big truck.

I tried to explain to her. "We don't have the room. We're out of space. We have to throw out the broken lamps and torn furniture and put the moldy books in the trash. We have to give away the food that's in the refrigerator, forget the big plants, give away the fertilizers and bags of grass seed and old and worthless tools."

It's a wonder Sandra and I didn't just have fatal strokes right on the spot.

Two hours before closing Sandra was in the basement pouring bottle after bottle of spoiled booze down the utility sink drain. Old wine, liqueurs, champagne, etc., stuff that was given to my parents and never opened. With no more room curbside, I was running around the city trying to find homes or empty dumpsters for the things I couldn't take or didn't want.

Believe it or not, all through this ordeal, my mother was fine. She never shed a tear or had a second thought about what she was doing. She turned her back and walked away from the house she had lived in for forty years as if it had meant nothing to her. Then again, she brought with her almost everything she had ever owned, including a collection of driftwood and olive wood stumps, and three boxes of rocks she had the movers pack for her. Yep, you read it right, she paid about a dollar per pound to move approximately 150 pounds of rocks from New York to Maine, a place where you almost can't take a step without tripping over a rock.

The house sold to a young surgeon and his pregnant wife. We had the closing at a law office in North White Plains and it was about as much fun as walking naked through a field of pucker brush. At one point, the buyer's agent insisted the dish washer in the house didn't work and that we would have to make an adjustment in the purchase price. Were they kidding me? They were buying a house with 35 year-old kitchen appliances. (The stove was much older.) Why should they care? They were planning to remodel the kitchen anyway.

Regardless, I knew the dishwasher worked. I said, "Fine. You go back to the house with Sandra and run the dishwasher. We'll wait here for your report."

So that's what we did, while his four attorneys and my one attorney sat together around the conference table and stared at one another. It was total foolishness.

Meanwhile, it took Sandra and this woman twenty minutes to get to the house, thirty minutes to run the dishwasher, and twenty minutes to come back. It cost me an hour. It cost him four hours.

Dishwasher worked perfectly.

The way I figure it, the buyer's agent cost that young surgeon and his wife about $2000 in legal fees. I hope to hell he took it out of her commission.

15. Time to See a New Doctor

My mother lived with us in our house for six months while her new house was being built next door. She adjusted to Maine, made new friends, joined the synagogue and the garden club, talked on the telephone to her friends in New York and wrote dozens of letters. She hooked up with a local doctor, got a new driver's license and a new automobile registration, learned to find her way to the grocery store and Walmart and, for the most part, adjusted to the move like a real trooper.

The new house was completed in January of 2003, and we moved everything out of storage and into the house in February. I had included a large basement in the original plans and most of the stuff we brought from New York ended-up there, boxed and taped shut. Only the rugs and furniture and valuables and essentials were unpacked and set up inside. I tried to maintain a minimalist attitude about the house. For a while, this worked to our benefit, as it gave my mother a lot to do, namely, opening boxes and looking to see what was inside. She would spend hours and hours in the basement opening and searching the contents of the boxes. It was like having a birthday party every day. Unfortunately, as you can imagine, what started out as a fun process would eventually turn into a frustrating chore and a source of aggravation and even anger. "The movers stole my [fill in the blank]."

The first year went really well, roughly from July 2002 to July 2003. She was happy and content. Even with the occasional persnickety little memory issues surfacing, she didn't seem lonely or have a need to dwell on the past. She hardly ever talked about my father, and when she did, she did so with affection and reason.

And then things started to unravel.

She got into the habit of telling people she had made the last move of her life. This refrain would eventually transmogrify into: "This is the last home I will ever live in." And finally to, "This is the house I will die in."

She slacked-off on her letter writing and started watching a lot more TV. She stopped making phone calls to her friends, and I started noticing strange telephone numbers on her phone bill and unusual charges on her credit card. Weird items showed up in the mail from the Shopping Network.

At synagogue she had trouble remembering the psalms and prayers she used to know so well. She would make up the words or just hum.

She took to taking long walks, very long walks. I would ask her to stay close to home and she would agree, but then she would just get to the end of the road and keep going. And yet, she always found her way home.

Late that first summer my aunt came to visit and stay with my mom at the house. During the visit, while the two of them were sitting on the porch together, my mom went on a rant about how she had a sister who never visited and who never called. It was clear to my aunt that my mom was talking about her without realizing it. She was, in truth, my mom's only living sister.

Another threshold reached.

Later that night, when we were alone together, my aunt asked me if I had ever had Mom tested. I said I had been thinking about it and had gotten the name of a neurologist in Portland.

Up to this point, everyone who knew my mom, her close family and friends, avoided the subject of her mental health. It was almost a taboo subject. Nobody wanted to be the first to say the words. It's as if there's a defense mechanism at play, or a denial reflex.

"How do you know she has dementia?"

"No, no way. It's the normal effects of aging."

And my favorite:

"I've been with your mother. I've never noticed anything like that."

16. The Neurologist

We drove to Portland, my mother, Sandra and I, in the hope of maybe combining a little shopping with the visit, maybe having a fancy lunch or dinner on the way home. The drive took two hours and on the way down my mother had to be reminded several times that we were going to the doctors and then to do some shopping.

Thinking back on this seminal visit, I'm a little fuzzy on the exact details. For example, I can't remember the time of day or whether she had already had her blood work and CAT scan, diagnostic procedures needed to rule out tumors, stroke or other root causes of her difficulties. I think probably we went to the neurologist first and after the visit we went straight to the diagnostic center for the additional procedures.

However, what I do remember is the pain and anguish of the verbal test the neurologist performed and the cold, calculating, detached and completely insensitive way in which it was performed.

My mother and I were both escorted into his office and introduced. He interviewed us briefly and then told my mother he would ask her some question and test her memory and ability to do some mental tasks. During this part of the exam I found myself making excuses for her:

"Oh, I'm not sure she's done any kind of math in a long, long time."

"She hasn't been reading the newspaper. She really doesn't know current events anymore."

"She has difficulty hearing and wears a hearing aid. You'll have to repeat the question louder."

"Oh, I don't think she would have ever answered a question like that."

What bothered me about the test right from the start was that it was a test. I hate tests. They're a challenge to a person's validity. This test is the worst test anyone will ever have to take. And they don't take it alone. Someone has to be there with them, and that someone is typically a loved one.

The first thing my mother had to do was remember a name and an address. The doctor told her he would ask her to recall this name and address at the end of the exam. She wasn't allowed to write it down. When the time came to recall this information she couldn't do it. Sadly, neither could I.

There were questions like:

"Who is the current President of the United States?"

"What is today's date?"

"What is the season of the year?"

He showed her pictures and simple drawings, bananas, apples, elephants, the White House, Mount Rushmore, things that she had to identify, and he asked her to perform simple tasks in her head. For example, she had to add and subtract numbers; count backwards from 100 and recite the months backwards starting in January.

Every time my mother faltered or failed to respond correctly felt like someone thrusting a long, sharp, kitchen knife into my chest.

Then came the clock test. He handed her a piece of paper on which was printed a clock with no hands. He asked her to draw in the hands for 4:30. She took the pen and paper and stared at it. Then she drew something on the paper that looked nothing like the hands of a clock.

I almost died.

Finally, in an ironic confirmation of society's and the medical community's bizarre relationship with the disease, I looked at the chart and saw that dementia and Alzheimer's were not the terms the neurologist wrote down. The official terms used were "Adult Mental Dysfunction."

Here we were, six years after my father had passed away, eight or ten years after he had told me, "Your mother can be difficult. Just wait, you'll see." Three years after almost everyone she knew had acknowledged a problem with her behavior and memory. And now, following an extensive neurological examination by a professional medical specialist -- and after having heard the painful truth of his diagnosis . . . we were still beating around the bush.

17. OK, It's Alzheimer's. Now What?

It wasn't like anything changed. Sandra and I knew what to expect from the doctor. We had already been living with my mother's issues and didn't really have to make any immediate adjustments. There was a new pill, namely, Aricept, but other than that, life in our small Maine town stayed much the same for a while.

Aricept (Donepizil) seemed to be the drug of choice for postponing the effect of Alzheimer's. It still is. There is another one, Namenda (Memantine). Some doctors will prescribe both, and others will use Aricept in the early stages and switch to Namenda later on.

Some doctors, and about 25% of nursing homes, will use psychoactive drugs like Risperdal, Seroquel, Zyprexa and Haldol to calm patients and make them more amenable. These drugs should never be used on people with Alzheimer's or any other form of dementia because they have been associated with an increased risk of suicide and other deaths. That said, my mother was put on Seroquel six months after she moved into a resident care facility in 2007, and the drug did indeed have a beneficial effect, for about one year. Unfortunately, the drug caused incredible weight gain (sixty pounds), and I believe it contributed to a stroke much later that left her catatonic for months.

When you read the drug manufacturers information about Aricept and Namenda you won't be very hopeful. Even the medical establishment views these two drugs, at best, as a means of slowing down the progression of the disease. Meanwhile, if you go on the Internet and read testimonials from family members whose loved ones are on these drugs, you'll come away with even less reason for optimism. For one thing, the manufacturers themselves will admit the drugs work on some people and not others, and, regardless of what they claim, the reality is there's virtually no way to tell how and if they are working.

Aricept is started at 5 mg and then after a two weeks it's marched up to 10 mg. The only noticeable change I witnessed in my mother was during the first night after the morning she had taken her first full-dose pill. That night she had what would best be described as a wakeful night terror. She woke up screaming and called me from next door. I ran to the house to find her shaking and in tears. As she described it, she woke up and turned around and saw herself lying in the bed asleep.

I called the doctor the next day, and he backed my mother down to 5 mg. She would remain on the 5 mg dose for about a month and then march back up to 10 mg. The second attempt to jump up to 10 mg worked without the night terrors or any other noticeable consequences.

At this point in her life my mother was taking three drugs. Aricept for her Alzheimer's and Norvasc and Toprol for her blood pressure. She also took vitamin supplements, particularly vitamin-e and all sorts of holistic, self-help products, the latter of which I could never get her to stop taking.

18. Are You Really Ready for The Sacrifice?

I had been forced to give up my job as captain of the
Penobscot Bay and River Pilot Boat when my mother
ended-up in the hospital with dehydration, but I was still
writing technical marine articles and working as a
professional boat captain and crewman for hire. One boat I
worked on semi-regularly was a three-hundred passenger
dinner boat in Rockland Harbor.

We had been working a weekend stretch for the Blues
Festival and were secure in our usual berth when I met a
woman on the fantail who had a lot to say about caring for
people with Alzheimer's.

She was an African-American woman about my age, from
the greater New Orleans area. We got to talking about a lot
of things and eventually it came up that my mother had just
been diagnosed with Alzheimer's.

"What are you going to do?" she said.

"I'm going to take care of her," I said.

"How many are you?"

"What do you mean?"

"I mean, is it just you?"

"My wife and I."

"Well, that's not enough," she said.

"I just built a house for her right next to us. We're going to move in there and take care of her," I said, feeling a bit perplexed.

The woman must have sensed my surprise. She moved her chair closer to me and looked me squarely in the eyes.

"I'm sorry to tell you this, and I mean no disrespect to you, your wife or your mother. I'm sure you're a loving son and quite capable. And I'm sure your mother is a lovely woman who wants nothing but the best for the two of you. But, unfortunately, it's just impossible for two people to care for a person with Alzheimer's. It would be hard for ten people. I can tell you this because my grandmother has Alzheimer's and we, the family, care for her. It's very, very hard, and there are over thirty of us. Do you work? Does your wife work?

"Yes, I said. "Both of us work. But I have a flexible schedule and I'll be able to take time off from work."

"For how long?" she said. "Sure, you can do it now, when all you have to do is cook and clean. But will you be able to do it for a year? Five years? Ten years? And who will entertain her. Who will care for her when she can no longer bathe or feed herself?"

A knot started tightening in my stomach.

"I hadn't thought of that," I said.

"I can tell you, there are over thirty of us, and it is very difficult. The scheduling. The sharing of the work load. The fact that not all of us can do what needs to be done. For example, none of the men can bathe her. None of the men can change her diapers. Some would do it, but my Grandmother is afraid of them."

"My mother will let me do it. I've bathed her already. I wasn't happy about it but I can do what needs to be done."

"That's very commendable. But will she want you to do it? Maybe she's OK with it now. Tomorrow, who knows."

A door was being slammed in my face, a big, black door with wrought iron chains and heavy steel padlocks.

"I guess I'll just have to do what I can do for as long as I can," I said.

"Forgive me for asking," she said. "And you don't have to tell me if you don't want to, but does your mother have the means to pay for her care?

"My father left her in good shape," I said. "She has a comfortable I.R.A."

"Then you're lucky," she said. "You have options."

19. The Line in the Sand

This woman from New Orleans and I talked into the night. Her advice would stay with me a long time and eventually turn out to be prophetic. The house I had built for my mother, the house she told people would be the last place in which she would ever live, the one I filled with all her belongings and memorabilia, including my father's collection of antiques and antiquities and my mother's art and art books, her paintings and sculptures, would soon become nothing more than a physical address full of meaningless stuff. Her needs would change in a dramatic and unforeseen way.

Even the woman I had met on the dinner boat did not prepare me for what was to happen next. Neither did the neurologist, who I would come to realize had no help to offer and who did virtually nothing other than use my mother -- and every other Alzheimer and dementia patient -- to gather statistical data, most likely for a pharmaceutical or government study that paid dividends or consulting fees to participating physicians. I resolved to end her treatment with the neurologist after a $270 visit where my mother did little more than sit with a cold-blooded technician who asked her questions that were read from a printed form. When we were "dismissed" from the neurologist's office and got into the car to drive home I could see just how severely these visits were agitating my mother. How would you feel if you were given a test once a month that you continued to fail time and time again, and each time you failed, the failure was worse than the one previous?

But it wasn't her memory or our concern for her safety that served as the catalyst for the next move. Sure, there was a burnt pot, a missed dose of medication and laundry soap in the dryer. There was a time or two when she wandered too far from home; I would get a telephone call from a friend telling me he'd seen my mother a mile or more from the house, headed in the wrong direction. Immediately I would jump in the truck to mount a rescue mission.

All these incidents took place, seemingly, in very short time. Mom went from being borderline self-sufficient to requiring constant supervision in about a month, and it wasn't any one particular event that triggered the changeover.

There was one afternoon she wandered into a neighbor's house and sat on the couch to watch TV with the couple's youngest son. One second the parents were upstairs listening to the TV downstairs. The next second they heard their son talking to someone. They ran downstairs and there was Mom, sitting on the couch as if she were in her own home. Was this the proverbial straw that broke the camel's back? Not quite. The changeover came more as a result of a sequence of events.

The car, of course, had ceased being an issue months earlier, by the end of her first summer here. She just stopped driving it, probably because it began to frighten her. She didn't need any coaxing to garage it, and we didn't discuss it or make an issue of it. We just quietly agreed I'd drive her wherever she needed to go. That part was easy, and it opened the door for me to be with her more and more.

More and more. Strange to think about it in these terms, but it is exactly this "more and more" that makes it so difficult for just two, three, four or even a half dozen people to serve as caregivers or supervisors to a family member suffering with Alzheimer's.

I was lucky with the car. Other families who find themselves in this situation, where a decision has to be made to take a person's keys from them, end up with a major crisis or an ongoing confrontation. In my case, I simply told her that the car was not really suitable for driving in the harsh Maine winters. She accepted it, and accepted her loss of car privileges.

More difficult for her and me was the access to outside companionship and social activities.

There was a woman friend of mine who hired herself out as a professional companion. She had some training in the health field and was quite the local socialite. I hired her on a weekly or biweekly basis to spend time with my mom. Occasionally, she would take my mom and a group of women or men and women to a concert or the beach or shopping. Sometimes she would just come over for lunch, or they would go to lunch and a museum together. It gave me the better part of a day to myself.

At one point, this person told me she had been catching my mom stealing stuff from the store. Little things that would find their way into her handbag. It reminded me of a Seinfeld episode. I think it's Jerry's uncle who gets caught and says to Jerry as a way of explaining: "We're old. They expect us to steal."

Another woman who used to chaperone my mom eventually had to stop this practice because my mom accused her of taking something from the house. This person was absolutely heartbroken until I explained that it was the illness at the root of the accusation and not my mother.

So, with these two incidents, suddenly her options for companionship and supervision were reduced by a factor of two. Two days more a week that I needed to spend with her.

There was also a call I got from her guitar teacher. She was having an impossible time keeping up in class, and her constant interruptions were making it too difficult for the teacher to do her job. A similar thing happened in synagogue with her singing the wrong hymns in a loud voice or her calling out inappropriately during the service. Add two more evenings and another afternoon to my watch.

No more guitar lessons. No more synagogue. No more shopping or museums with a paid or volunteer companion. No more garden club. No more visits from Dr. M. or her sister. (They would both visit her a year or so later at a resident care facility.) No more planned activities without me or Sandra in accompaniment.

Then came two admissions from my mother that literally floored me. And believe me when I say this: I wish this was exaggeration.

The first one hit out of the blue when I was talking to her about not walking so far from the house.

"Mom," I said. "How can you walk so far away from the house? What if you have to use the bathroom."

"Well," she said. "I'll just knock on someone's door."

"What if they're not home?" I said.

"I just go around back."

"What do you mean?"

"I did it once. I went around the back of the house."

Oh Jesus!

"Ma, you can't do that."

"Why not? Nobody saw me."

"How do you know?"

"Because I know."

Of course you do.

Lastly, there was this one morning I stopped by the house to check on her. At this point, she was either with me on my errands, or I was staying in the house and working in the guest room, or I was in and out of the house a dozen times a day.

"Bob," she said. "I had that nice dog in the house today. I've been feeding him for a couple of weeks now."

"Riley?" I said. "No way. He's an outdoor dog. He's probably covered in tics and flees." This flabbergasted me because my mother had gotten into the habit of sometime not letting my dog into the house. My dog was always clean as a whistle.

"Who's Riley?" she said.

"The big chocolate lab from up the street. Not to mention he's always got some kind of bowel problem."

"What does he look like?"

"I don't know, Ma. He's either a chocolate lab or a German pointer. I can't remember. He's dark and he has short hair and he's fat."

"No, no. This dog has long hair and he's not fat. He's very sweet. I've been giving him cheese every day."

She used to give cheese to my dog.

"Fine, Ma. Whatever. Don't let him in the house anymore. He's dirty. OK?"

She placated me with an "If you think so, dear." But I could tell she thought I was being unreasonable.

The next day was a Saturday. And I think it was one of the last days she would go to synagogue with one of her friends. They picked her up at about 9:00 in the morning. I took off from my house to go on a boat run and as I was driving by her house I looked down the driveway and noticed a pile of fur on the walkway by her front door. I hit the brakes, then backed up so I could see the furry thing more clearly.

It was a sixty or seventy pound coyote fifteen or twenty feet from my mother's front door. Biggest, most beautiful coyote I had ever seen. And why not? It was getting fat on cheddar cheese, hot dogs and leftover Chinese food.

I pulled in the driveway and opened the door of the truck. As I took a step toward the animal it got up and headed for the corner of the house. It was looking at me over its shoulder as it sauntered off. I went around the other side of the house and met it in the back yard. I whistled and told it to go away. It sped up and trotted into the woods. I never saw it at my mother's house again. However . . .

It was the winter of 2010, three years after my mother had moved to a resident care facility, and I was snow-blowing the driveway of Sandra's house during a particularly bad winter storm. I had this sixth sense there was something or somebody behind me. I turned around and came face-to-face with a scraggly, half-starved, mangey-looking coyote standing twenty feet away. It had the same coloring as the one my mother had been feeding for two weeks.

Of course, I have no way of knowing if it was the same coyote, but the way it looked at me, with its soulful, pained, hungry eyes, made me think that if it could talk, it would have asked:

"Where's your Mom?"

20. Day Care

By now, August of 2006, my mother was spending virtually every minute of the day with me, except at night when she went to sleep in her own house. She was also getting ready for bed very early, sometimes as early as 4:30 in the afternoon. I'm not sure if she did this because she was depressed and had nothing interesting to do, or because she had completely lost track of time.

At night, when Sandra and I finished work, we would have her over for dinner and some TV-watching. Invariably, after about 15 minutes of watching something on TV, she would ask, "What are we going to do now?"

I would say: "We're doing it, Ma. Just watching a little TV."

She would nod, but fifteen minutes later she would ask the question again.

This is when I first started to realize she needed so much more than personal care and attention. When people talk to you about the needs of someone with Alzheimer's, they talk mostly about making sure the person is comfortable and safe from harm. They don't usually talk about keeping them entertained. But think about it. When you lose your ability to keep track of time, it must seem like time comes to a standstill, or nearly to a standstill. With time crawling, one minute might seem like an hour or longer. The boredom becomes palpable.

A sane, normal person with a normal functioning brain can't possibly understand what a person with Alzheimer's is feeling. Conversely, if we have a loved one who is suffering from a pain due to a malignancy, we can sort of appreciate what they are going through. We all have experienced pain at one time or another. We have had broken bones or gotten burned. We have had kidney stones, earaches, toothaches, etc. We have contracted infections, viral and bacterial. Some have had cancer and other very serious and painful diseases. We can relate to physical pain. We can relate to not having any energy. But how can we relate to not knowing the passage of time? How can we relate to feelings of chronic boredom due to a type of self-inflicted time dilation? What happens to a person with Alzheimer's does not come and go like other maladies. It's not something that can afflict a healthy person, and then after a while that person gets better and can now say: "Oh yeah, I had that once, it was horrible. I know what you're going through."

Strangely, in its own weird way, my mother's inability to watch thirty minutes of television without getting bored got me to broach the subject of her maybe finding a place where she would have more activity. She asked me what kind of place, and I suggested we look around. I mentioned the words "Assisted Living" for the first time. Much to my surprise, she responded enthusiastically to the idea.

As a matter of course, it was impractical and inadvisable for us to visit Assisted Living facilities without my going to them and checking them out beforehand. At her stage of mental dysfunction she would need to go into a lock-down situation. But her cognitive awareness was still enough for her to want much more freedom than those places allowed. She would see the unlocked part of the Assisted Living area, with it's apartment-like accouterments, and would want to live there. Also, she wasn't yet at the stage where she needed help with her personal bathing and hygiene. And many of the lock-down or Alzheimer's Care Units in the larger facilities had rooms without showers. They had a washroom on the floor to which the resident would be escorted and, if needed, helped through the process of bathing and washing. This was not the type of facility my mother would go to voluntarily.

I visited four facilities in the area. All were larger institutions that had a parent organization and an unlocked and locked area for residents. I took brochures and brought them back for my mother to review, but in truth I did not really like any of these facilities. There were very few private rooms and hardly any of the rooms had private showers. Moreover, when I toured the four closest places I was struck by the fact that not much of anything was going on. Residents had been plopped in front of televisions and I did not see a lot of staff doing anything more than what Sandra and I were doing.

One day we tried an Alzheimer's day care center that was being run by one of the facilities in the midcoast area. I drove my mother down and went in with her. We entered a single recreation room with six to ten people in it. Two women introduced themselves as staff. My gut reaction was not very positive. I didn't perceive a high degree of professionalism or training, and none of the elderly men and women there seemed to be participating in any kind of formal activity. It all appeared ad hoc and disorganized. Nevertheless, I kissed my mom goodbye, told her I'd see her in a couple hours, and left.

It was a singularly difficult moment for me for obvious reasons. After all, I had just left my mother in day care. Day care! What about placing a mother or father in day care makes any sense in a normal world?

I drove around town for three hours until it was time to pick her up. When she got in the car and I looked at her face I knew we wouldn't be going back.

"How was it?" I asked.

"All right, I guess," she said.

It wasn't. I could tell.

"Did you meet anyone interesting?"

"There was a gentleman there who invented something."

Actually, the man had founded and run a chain of well-established retail stores in Maine and New England. He now had Alzheimer's and spent his days playing with crayons and coloring books.

On the drive home I started wondering what was going through my mother's mind. Did she realize she would soon be playing with coloring books? Did she know what was coming? Was she afraid of it? A year or two earlier, she had mentioned to me that she wanted to take a pill to end it all. Did she still feel that way, or had the Alzheimer's created in her another reality I couldn't quite comprehend?

A few days later, while I was on a short errand, my mother walked into the neighbor's house and sat down on the couch with the couple's youngest son. The couple were upstairs and heard voices and came down and there was my mom on the couch watching TV with their son.
Fortunately, we live in a wonderful little neighborhood in coastal Maine. While it can be said that people who live here have been hardened by cold winters and rough Yankee traditions, one simple fact remains:

When put to the test, Mainers can be the kindest, most helpful people in the world.

21. Finding the Right Alzheimer's Care Facility

I started calling around the state of Maine and ended-up visiting three facilities. Two would accept my mother and one said she had gone beyond the stage that met their qualifications for admittance, which is to say that even though she could still bathe and wash herself and take care of most of her immediate physical needs, she could not be trusted to evacuate the building without supervision. The former two facilities were set up dorm room style, with a separate bathing area and strict restrictions regarding what personal items you could bring in, while the latter one was more of an intermediate assisted living facility. In other words, it provided minimal supervision and very little skilled care. I wasn't particularly interested in any of them. My mother wasn't going to a place where she would have to walk through the halls to take a bath, and she couldn't go into a place that wasn't locked down.

Once you start looking around you will be amazed at the great diversity of plans and options, in terms of both care and costs. For example, some facilities allow personal belongings and furnishings and others don't. Some allow powered scooters. Some don't. The Area Agency on Aging for the Capitol Area (AACAP), which can be found at aaacap.org, provides a very good breakdown of what you're likely to find once you start looking. (See Appendix: Part A for more information.)

For the most part, the selection runs the gamut. At one end of the spectrum there are unlicensed, converted private homes with shared or private rooms, paid for monthly. These can and do offer many adults excellent end-of-life alternatives. They may be found in cities, suburbs or even beautiful country settings. However, the special care needed to house people with Alzheimer's and other types of acute mental dysfunction requires a level of staffing, training and licensing these places typically don't provide.

At the other end, there are the transitional assisted living to continuous care operations. These start a resident in an assisted living environment and then transition him or her from, say, an apartment, into full time nursing care as the need arises. Some are paid for with a security deposit and a monthly rent check. Others may require an upfront investment or buy-in of many thousands of dollars.

In the middle are the licensed assisted living facilities that provide supervised care but not nursing care, and the facilities that provide continuous nursing care but offer none of the accouterments of an assisted living environment.

My personal search left me underwhelmed by the facilities in my immediate area. The first place I visited had a dorm-style layout and didn't allow personal furniture. During my tour of the Alzheimer's wing, the staff were gathered in the kitchen while the residents sat unsupervised in front of the TV. One of the residents, a younger man, was interacting excitedly with the others around him. He seemed to be annoying his housemates. These and other observations at this facility didn't leave me feeling warm and fuzzy.

The second place I visited had beautiful grounds and luxurious accommodations. It also had a buy-in fee of $40,000.

The other facilities I called in Maine either didn't have a room available or they were in a part of the state that might as well have been in Australia.

22. If I Knew Then What I Know Now

I'm not exactly sure how I found the place but it was probably by way of a Google search on the Web and a follow-up phone call. The facility was in Concord, New Hampshire. It had a section with apartments for people who could come and go as they please, and it had a smaller section of apartments designated for people with Alzheimer's Disease and other forms of adult mental dysfunction. This other, smaller section, had locked outer doors and it's own open air courtyard. However, even though the Alzheimer's/Dementia Care section was locked and separate from the main facility, the residents shared some types of programming, particularly evening programs and special events for families.
I made the first trip to Concord myself, met with the various staff people and took a tour of the place. I liked how residents had their own full bathrooms and their own little kitchen area. I especially liked that residents could bring in their own furniture.

One should remember that all these places are run as businesses, and there's a tendency to forget the realities and nuances of what people do when they're trying to drum up business. Don't get me wrong here. I'm not trying to be unfair or unkind, nor am I trying to be critical of the way the system works. But there's a point to be made, which is that people trying to get your business will often say things or promise things they can't really deliver.

For example, when my mother decided this was where she wanted to be, and I started going through the application and registration process, I was assured more than once that the facility could handle a person's end of life needs. Most places will tell you this. They will tell you they can take your loved one from assisted living, into and through continuing care, and finally into hospice or whatever it is you have chosen for the last days of your life.

But this is only half the story. The truth is the vast majority of residential care facilities are not equipped to handle residents who need continuing care. What they mean when they say they can provide continuing care is that they will continue to provide a place for your loved one to live but that the additional care will be provided by you, financially and otherwise. You will need to supply and pay for private nursing and even, possibly, an additional personal caregiver.

One clue as to the veracity of a facility's claims is the facility itself. If you tour the home and see that every room is carpeted, you can bet they are not going to be providing continuing care at their expense. If you walk through the facility and there are no wheelchairs, oxygen tanks, medical carts, hospital-like beds or people with bandages or special treatment needs, there is no continuing care.

Facilities that can take a person full term have a separate area for full time nursing care. They have wheelchairs and other equipment for people who are non-ambulatory. If a resident can no longer get our of bed by themselves, they won't be lifted out of bed by a Norwegian bodybuilder named Ingrid. They will be lifted with a special hoist, and then, typically, placed in a special chair. If neither of these things are visible when you tour the facility, then you will have to provide them, one way or another.

Another point to consider is feeding. Ask the facility if they will feed your loved one when your loved one can no longer feed themselves. You will probably be surprised at the answer. Sure, they will feed your loved one, but you will be paying extra for a caregiver to come in at least three times a day.

The thing to remember is that most all resident care facilities are designed in the same way. They're built to offer the resident the greatest degree of freedom and as close to a homelike experience as can be made possible, for as long as the resident can manage in the environment provided. To accomplish this they minimize the hospital or nursing home feel, and in so doing function by providing limited basic care, which means there is one staff person who will be helping your loved one out of bed, helping them get dressed, helping them get washed or ready for meals and programming. The minute your loved one needs two staff people, the equation changes. In addition, most resident care facilities do not have highly trained staff to help with feeding. They use PCAs or CNAs (Personal Care Assistants or Certified Nurses Aids) and not LPNs or RNs. A PCA does not have anywhere near the training of an LPN or RN, and they may not be equipped to handle a person who suddenly swallows incorrectly.

Furthermore, your average resident care facility is staffed with only one or two LPNs, and usually only during the day. At night, they may be on call from home.

I started this chapter with the heading "If I Knew Then What I Know Now," which implies that I would have done things differently given the benefit of twenty-twenty hindsight. Truth is, I'm not sure I could have done anything different. Sure, it would have been wonderful if my mother could have transitioned from her apartment in the resident care facility to a room and bed in a continuing care facility without having to experience the shock of an ambulance ride and a move to a completely different building. It would have been so much better for her to have taken a few meals in the nursing home section and then returned to her apartment at night, done it like this for a few days or a month to make the transition less traumatic. But this isn't how it's done. Most importantly, my mother would not have wanted to move into a large facility knowing the facility had a "secret" wing in which there were people waiting for death.

In any event, I liked this place in Concord, N.H., and after my visit, I came home with brochures and pamphlets and gave them to my mom. She looked them over and got excited about the prospect of moving to a place where she would be inspired and kept active. Maybe it was the next day or the day after or a week after that, I can't remember. Either way, at some point we drove to Concord together and she had a chance to tour the place herself. She liked it and said she was ready to make the move. I asked her if she was sure and she said she was.

Just like that. An era ended.

23. The Last Long Road Trip She Would Ever Take

The night before we were scheduled to leave for her new home I found a Honer harmonica she had bought in Switzerland for me when I was just a little kid. It was in the drawer in her night stand next to the bed. She did that. She kept things of my brother's and mine in odd paces. Little reminders of us. My harmonica. A Thunderbird toy of my brother's. All these things had been kept close to her in drawers or cabinets. Almost everyplace in the house where something could be stored, a keepsake of some type had been hidden. The basement was a treasure trove of useless junk. I think every clay handprint we made in kindergarden was down there, as was the karate uniform I had when I was nine years old. My old cub scout uniform. The list goes on and on.

It was January 10, 2007, about 8:00 in the evening. I had just finished packing everything up in the U-Haul trailer. I closed the door of the trailer and went back in the house. We needed to get an early start the next morning because I had to drive her and her furniture and other belongings, including a change of clothes for a month, to New Hampshire, and I had to unload everything and move her and her stuff into her new apartment.

Before I left her house I took the harmonica and slid it into my breast pocket, then I kissed her goodnight and told her I would be waking her early at 6:00 AM. She seemed calm and relaxed. If she had any doubts or trepidation I was not aware of it. Conversely, I was a wreck.

I walked the 500 feet back to the house in which Sandra and I lived and collapsed on the couch. I thought about my mother down the road, with my truck and a U-Haul full of her bedroom furniture sitting in the driveway, and her trying to sleep in the guest bedroom. What was she thinking? Was she nervous? Was she upset about all this? How did she feel about me sending her away when she had made me promise so long ago to never place her in a nursing home?

Before I knew it, I was blowing notes on the harmonica. I never did learn how to play the damn thing, although, as a kid, I played it a lot, which is maybe why it meant so much to my mother. She had bought it for me, and I apparently had loved it. Must have made her incredibly happy to give me something that brought me so much joy, enough so that she would keep it in a drawer in her night stand next to the bed.

I still couldn't play a song. Just random notes. Kind of like the notes Charles Bronson's character plays in the movie, Once Upon a Time in the West. How apropos. The character in the movie played the notes to lament the loss of his father at the hands of a ruthless, land-grubbing thug. In my case, it wasn't a thug that caused my lamentations and torment. It was simply the roll of the dice. Life. But maybe not any less ruthless.

We left early Thursday morning, and I had my mom moved in by 2:30 in the afternoon. I wasn't sure what to expect when it came time for me to leave. I knew I was going to be traumatized and depressed but had no idea what to expect from her. Would she break down, ask me to stay, beg me not to leave her?

I waited for dinner. When she started for one of the tables I kissed her on the cheek and said I'd see her later. She said OK and sat down with two other ladies. Before I slipped out the door, I looked back to see how she was coping. She was talking up a storm.

On the way home, a loose wire in the trailer shorted out several fuses in my truck. I had no lights. I replaced the fuses only to have them blow again, then I noticed my alternator wasn't charging. Truck was completely dead an hour later. I had to get a tow for both my truck and the trailer (tow cost $500) and didn't get home until 3:30 in the morning on Friday. That was a bad day, a really bad day. The truck slowly dying on the road, headlights getting dimmer and dimmer, panel indicators blinking on and off for no apparent reason, heater motor fading, it was all so damned metaphorical. And yet, the breakdown was probably a Godsend. Even now, the memory of the whole affair overshadows the terrible sense of loss and failure I had on the ride back from Concord.

I went to visit her again on Saturday. I arrived at 1:30 and stayed until 3:30. It was an illuminating experience, to say the least. She looked great, and the staff loved her. She had had her nails painted. I mentioned how good they looked and she said it had taken her all day to do them. When I mentioned how good they looked a second time, she said that one of the girls there had painted everyone's nails.

Mom didn't really know she was in a health care facility. She thought she was in her own home, surrounded by all her own things. I can't explain it but she was relaxed and at ease, comfortable in her surroundings. It was as if when she was out in the real world she was spending every second of the day fighting the disease, fighting to maintain some sense of reality. And she was being haunted by the things she and my dad had accumulated over their forty-six years of marriage, things that had memories she wanted so much to recall but couldn't. At the same time, she was fighting minute by minute to not screw up, to not make a mistake or be a burden on me or anyone else. But now she was in a different place, a place where she could let go and be herself. She was free to let the disease take her.

On Saturday, I didn't know how to leave. I asked her if I should go, and she said it was OK to stay, that I could stay as long as I wanted. I just said OK. But then one of the staff members was starting a sing-a-long and my mom wanted to take part in it. She went over to participate and I just kissed her on the cheek and let her go. I asked one of the PCAs if I should just leave and she said I could do whatever I wanted. She said I could go over and say goodbye again, or have my mom walk me to the door (it's a lock down facility with a coded key pad door lock), or I just leave. It's not really be a big deal, she said. The residents seem to accept this place as their home.

I opted to leave. If my mom asked for me, the nurse said she would tell her I had to go and that I would be back later.

I found a little Chinese/Japanese restaurant at the end of town, had some sake, a spicy tuna roll, hamachi nigiri, and a soft shell crab tempura. My appetite was back. The previous Thursday, the day I moved her in and the night my truck broke down, I hadn't eaten a thing. Not much on Friday, either. I had never even gotten hungry. For me, that's highly unusual.

Sunday, the Patriots beat San Diego by a field goal.

I can't say I was happy when I left but I can say that I knew deep down inside it was the right thing to do.

At least that was how I felt then.

24. Major Life Changes

The ride to Concord from my home took three hours and fifteen minutes if I didn't stop for gas or food and four hours if I did. I got into the habit of making the trip two days a week for the first month or two and then I dropped it back to one day a week. If I could I would squeeze in another trip. The travel usually averaged out to going every five days.

On rare occasions I would get there and she would be starting a field trip or a program or special event. This happened at least half a dozen times and when it did I would kiss her on the cheek and turn around and come home. Believe it or not these were the best visits because I knew she was happy and didn't need me for her emotional well being. More often than not I would get there and we would sit in the courtyard or take part in a program of some kind of activity. Some times I would take her out for a drive.

When I would walk through the door and see my mother she would look around the room at the others and exclaim, "My son. My son is here." She always seemed to have a smile, and the staff loved her. They told me she awoke in the morning singing and dancing, which is something she used to do all the time, even after my father had died.

But then my wife's youngest son, Daniel, died. And although one thing had absolutely nothing to do with the other, and my mother was never told about Daniel, it seemed like things started to change for her. Part of that change was due to a drug called Seroquel.

Daniel died six months to the day that my mother went into the residential care facility. He had been struggling with drugs, and the fight had taken its toll on everyone. But as painful as the struggle and the handling of his situation was, all of us would endure it again if it meant we could have him back for just one day. Because as hard as it was living with a drug addict for three years, the shock of opening the door to a police officer bearing that kind of bad news was one hundred times worse. And what followed, the grief and sense of failure, was nearly debilitating.

There are some weird parallels between what happened with Daniel and what happened with my mother. Daniel was an addict for three years. My mother was in Alzheimer's residential care for three years. Daniel stopped thinking of his family. My mother stopped thinking of her family. Daniel said and did things without considering the consequences. My mother did the same. And when they both died, they left behind a deep emotional hole and a lot of self-doubt.

I stayed home that month that Daniel died. And when I finally got back to Concord, there had been a change in my mother's behavior. I don't mean a drastic, 180-degree about-face change, because she had exhibited similar behavior even before she moved to Concord. The difference now was that the resident care director, with both her doctor's and my approval, decided to manage my mother's behavior with a "happy" drug.

Long before my mother moved to Concord she had become obsessed with other people's weight. If she passed someone at the grocery store or on the street who was overweight or, God forbid, obese, she would blurt out something to the effect: "Oh my, she's so fat! She needs to lose weight!" And she would say these things loud enough for everyone to hear.

Unfortunately as her disease progressed, these observations and exclamations became more pronounced and more frequent. It happens with Alzheimer's and dementia. The person's vocabulary, communication skills, and inner compass begin to erode. Soon they have no inhibitions or boundaries. If they're alone or among family, it's manageable, but in a public setting or a nursing home, it can be a problem, especially when you have people at various stages of mental dysfunction.

When you're in a group home, and you're very overweight, and someone looks at you and then turns around and says: "Oh my God, she's so fat!" And this happens every day, day after day, and it's the only thing this person says to you or about you . . . obviously this is not an ideal way to go through your few remaining days or months.

Let me add, because it may or may not be relevant, that the Licensed Nurse who served as the resident care director just happened to be fat.

So why did I approve the drug?

I approved the drug because the doctor said it was safe and because (1) we were starting with an almost imperceptible dose and (2) I had no choice. My mother's behavior had become intolerable in group settings.

In retrospect, my mother's behavior should have been addressed psychotherapeutically. She should have been given time to work with professionals and specialists who have experience in these matters. The pharmaceutical option should have been an absolute last resort, and I'm not sure it was. But, as I said before, assisted living facilities are designed to provide residents with a homelike environment and as much freedom as possible. They're mostly staffed with PCAs and usually only one LPN. There are no doctors, no therapists, no psychologists. And, at the time, Seroquel was commonly prescribed to elderly patients in these situations. Twenty-nine percent of Seroquel was being prescribed to geriatric patients.

So, my mother was given Seroquel, a "happy" drug with a less than stellar reputation. (It's no longer recommended for patients with any form of dementia.) Over time, her dose was boosted to 100 mg. A small dose, really, when you consider that a schizophrenic or somebody with a severe sleep or bipolar disorder might be prescribed as much as 800 or 1,000 mg. Nevertheless, the drug worked. She was a lot less agitated, and she stopped insulting the care director and the other overweight residents.

If you're detecting sarcasm and bitterness here it is for good reason. My mother was placed on the drug April 17, 2007, about three months after she moved into her new apartment at the assisted living facility. Granted, it was a small dose, and in the beginning it had virtually no effect on her, except to make her a little more calm and less intrusive to others, but I think in the long run it was a bad drug, a very bad drug.

Naturally, I blame myself, because I was her last line of defense. I approved the drug and the dosage increases based on the advice of the resident care director, my mother's doctor and research I had done on my own. What the heck? Everybody was using it in clinics and nursing homes around the world. Seroquel was (and still is) a $2 billion a year industry.

Talk about screwed-up timing. She went on the drug in April. In June, Daniel died. Even though I called the home frequently to check on her reaction and progress to the drug, I didn't get back to see her until the middle of July. We were grieving for Daniel and it was hard to leave, impossible to leave. By the time I got back to see her and check on things enough time had elapsed -- she had been on the drug for three months -- that I had no accurate means of establishing a baseline.

That's one of the strange things about Alzheimer's. You can't tell when it's the disease or something else. In other words, how can you really tell Aricept is helping? Namenda? Or any other drug? How do you measure the effectiveness of an anti-psychotic medication like Seroquel? How will you notice a barely perceptible and potentially dangerous side effect? The answer. You probably won't. Because nobody can say for sure what the natural course of the Alzhemier's deterioration is going to be with a given individual. And a person with Alzhemer's can't tell you what's wrong. It's a guessing game.

Ultimately, my mother gained sixty pounds while on Seroquel. She remained on the drug for one year and ten months, and I believe it was responsible for a stroke that left her catatonic and eventually precipitated her move to full-time nursing care. Furthermore, I think Seroquel might have had something to do with the physical torture she endured for the six months that preceded her death.

25. The Balancing Act

After what seemed like an appropriate amount of time had elapsed following Daniel's death I started going to Concord twice a week. I figured I needed to make up for lost time and check my mother's response to the Seroquel. What I found when I got there was that she seemed happy. She started each day with smiles, song, laughter and unbridled enthusiasm. She walked around the halls (there were only two) and often visited with other residents in their apartments. She participated in the activities and programs with gusto, and the staff appreciated her good humor and positive attitude.

This shouldn't give you the idea that my visits were pleasurable. On the contrary, every visit brought a new and different kind of sadness. Day by day she lost more cognitive and communication skills, and her ability to remember the people and events from her past had disappeared entirely. Her sister came to visit and she didn't recognize her or know who was sitting with her the entire time. And while she recognized my brother when he came to see her, she didn't know anything about his wife or her four grandchildren.

Over the years, through her late forties and fifties, she had created sculptures and paintings that had fetched thousands of dollars from appreciative art lovers. Now she made paper hats and proudly displayed pages torn out of coloring books. She could no longer play Bingo or participate in any program that required associative thinking. And the Seroquel, which helped keep the group home a contented place, added to her waistline and took away her motor skills day by day and week by week. Less steady on her feet, she would soon require the aid of a walker to get around.

During her residency at the Alzheimer's home, a total of about three years, she got ill with flu-like symptoms once or twice and fell more than a few times. The falls ranged from just sliding off her bed onto her keister to keeling over and landing square on her face and torso. After one fall she ended-up with two black eyes. It's easy at times like these to place blame on the professional care at the facility, but the simple fact is, it can't ever meet your expectations if your expectations are unreal from the start. You have to keep telling yourself, these places are trying to give your loved one as much freedom as possible. They're trying to extend quality of life. Would you rather they have your loved one strapped in a chair or restricted to a chair under constant supervision?

Admittedly, it's very disheartening and frustrating to find out your mother has taken a fall that has left her with two black eyes. But you have to put it in perspective.

When my mother was under my care, the following had happened:
She became dehydrated from not drinking enough and had collapsed on her front lawn. This occurred despite my trying to push fluids to her daily.

Even while under my careful watch, and long before she had gone into supervised care, she had fallen. She had taken falls while living with me and Sandra, while visiting my brother, and while living alone. She could fall while standing or walking just a few feet away from any one of us.

She dislocated her finger at Sandra's house while pulling up her pants.

She walked into the neighbor's house uninvited and sat down to watch TV. And not to forget she had entertained a wild coyote in her living room.

She got lost on long walks and I would have to go get her and drive her home.

One time on a visit I decided to take her for a stroll around the resident care facility. She was in a wheelchair at this point. It was our first experience with the wheelchair. As we stepped outside the front doors, my dog escaped the leash and headed for the parking lot. I momentarily let go of the chair to retrieve the dog and the chair took off with my mother in it. I had neglected to set the brakes. The chair went over the curb and I got there just in time to avoid a nasty accident. I threw myself under the chair and caught my mother as she fell sideways over the curb.

Another time, Sandra, my mom and I were sitting in the courtyard, my mom in the middle. A hornet flew into the picture. It circled in a threatening manner. I remember how nice my mother looked. She had on this colorful open blouse. I guess the hornet was attracted to the color, because that's where it wanted to be. I moved to shoo the hornet away and the damn thing stung my mother right on her breast.

The point is, you strive to give a person as much freedom as they can handle, and then when something triggers a change, you make the change. For example: The car.

A person's right to drive is a big deal. And it becomes a traumatic change of venue when an individual is told they can no longer drive. This is particularly true for a man. Take away your father's or grandfather's car keys and you open the door for a major confrontation. So you give them some room, some flexibility, until something significant happens, and I don't mean little bumps and bruises that appear almost out of nowhere.

In my mother's case, the car thing went by with unexpected ease. I told her the car wasn't suitable for the harsh Maine winters and that the snow and salt would hasten it's demise from rust and corrosion. I said we should store it through the winter and I volunteered to drive her everywhere she needed to go. Fortunately for me, by the time summer arrived, she didn't seem that interested in driving. It was as if she had become a little scared of it. And no wonder. She had been having difficulties with her car long before relocating to Maine, and this was in an area she had been living in for about forty years.

In New York she had accidentally closed the automatic garage door on the roof of the car, just missing the moon roof. She regularly clipped the side view mirrors and had more than her fair share of scrapes with parking curbs and parking meters. The worst, probably, was that time she stopped to get directions from a bunch of cops engaged in a deadly shootout.

My mother loved her car, and she continued to drive for two years after moving to Maine. But I think she knew, on her own, when the time had come for her to give up her keys. Disregarding the previous difficulties, the area she now found herself demanded a new set of driving skills. And after she moved to Concord, it became a total non-issue. Before the end of her first year in Concord she would have no memory of her car, or that she ever had a driver's license.

Basically, when it comes to safety and preservation versus freedom and dignity, it's a balancing act. You, as the family caregiver, have to play the balancing act. So do the professional caregivers and the professional care institutions. I think you can only hold these places accountable for just so much. They can't prevent illness. They can't prevent a person from taking an accidental fall. Not completely.

26. Redirection and Lying

When you spend time with people who have Alzheimer's you learn very quickly what to say and not say. You learn how to act and not act. For example:

You don't tell people with Alzheimer's all the things that have happened to you and your extended family. My mother was never told of Daniel's death, nor was she informed of any other deaths or health issues with any other family members.

You don't talk about what you did today or yesterday. You don't mention your vacations or what's going on with the old neighborhood and the old house. You don't talk about people from the past.

You don't ask questions like:

"What did you do today (or yesterday), Mom?"

Or,

"Sarah says hello. Remember Sarah?"

You don't correct them, ever, or talk about Alzheimer's or dementia.

You don't bring your troubles, your worries or your cares to them.

Instead, you walk in with a huge smile. You laugh. You makes jokes. You live and interact in the moment, from one minute to the next.

You also learn about redirection and lying. What's redirection? It's when you nudge a person with Alzheimer's or dementia in another direction by changing the subject or creating a diversion. For example, when your mother starts going on and on about the person across the room being fat, and she keeps talking about it and can't stop, you show her a magazine with a picture of Sean Connery and say: "He's a handsome guy, isn't he?"

Lying is self-explanatory. But here's an example anyway: When you tell your mother you're going to head home and she asks if she can come back with you, you say: "Well, I don't have room in the car right now because it's full of equipment from a job, but how about tomorrow? How about I pick you up tomorrow?" And she says OK, but fifteen minutes later you know she won't remember anything about it or the fact that you had no intention of taking her anywhere.

Or you get ready to leave and she asks you where you're going and you say, I was going to head home. And she says, why don't you use the guest room upstairs? And you answer, "Great, I think I will. Thanks, Ma. See you in the morning." And you kiss her goodbye. Then you get in your car and drive home.

As I mentioned earlier, it didn't take long for my mother's sphere of knowledge and awareness to collapse into a radius that covered her new place of residence and its courtyard. After three months, it was her home, and it had always been her home. As far as she knew, I was living upstairs. She had no knowledge of her old house in New York, her new house in Maine, or any of the exotic places she had been to in her life.

Meanwhile, as uncomfortable as it was to have my mother ask to go back with me, and as much as I wanted her not to do it, a year later I would have given almost anything for one more chance to say, "Yes, get your stuff and get it the car." Because the point at which she stopped asking to go with me was also the point at which she stopped asking questions altogether.

27. Giving-in to Professional Care

Whenever my mother wasn't taking part in some formal programming I would take her out for a ride or a walk around the grounds. Our conversations were limited to the weather and scenery or how she was feeling. The only things we could talk about were things we could see and touch.

By my mother's second year at the resident care facility she and I were spending our time together just sitting next to one another. We hardly spoke. Not soon afterwards, the year before she was to leave the facility to go to the nursing home, she started to call me, "Mommy" or "Mother." Sometimes I got the feeling she thought I was my dad and other times I was sure she thought it was her mother holding her hand or lying next to her in her bed. But then an aide would give her a nudge and ask, "Judy, who's that?" And she would answer, "My son." It was all very unpredictable.

Those were some of the better visits. I would get there, exhausted, at around 2:00 in the afternoon. I'd walk in and sit and watch TV with her and the other residents, or we would go into the courtyard and sit together on a bench. We would sit like that for a half hour to an hour and watch the chipmunks. On rare occasions I would find her in her clothes resting on top of the bedcovers. I would lie down next to her on the bed. Sometimes she would reach over and grab my hand. One time she rolled over and rested her head on my shoulders and slept like a baby. At least I have these visits to look back on.

I also have the bad visits to look back on. The singular visits, the ones that changed everything that came afterwards. One time I walked into the Alzheimer's wing as

I had one hundred times before. I said hello to everyone and asked about my mom's whereabouts. One of the aides said she was probably in her room. When I walked in I found her on the bed wallowing in her own feces. She was totally disoriented and confused, pushing at the covers and trying to figure out where she was and what had happened. She had feces on her face. I immediately called one of the aides and she and another girl got my mother up and in the shower. They stripped the bed completely, opened the windows and threw everything in the wash. This visit was a major turning point, and it left me with a very bad feeling about the future.

A professional caregiver once described the disease to me as follows:

When we're born, our world (or sphere of awareness) is confined to what we can see and touch. It extends to a point just beyond our fingertips. As we grow and our senses develop our world starts to expand. Fully matured, our world extends to the stars and beyond. We are confined only by the limits of our imaginations.

As Alzheimer's Disease progresses, and our mental capabilities deteriorate, our world shrinks again. We first retreat from our memories of the distant past and our general knowledge of places, things, people and words. We retreat next from our immediate past, including schedules, dates and finally pieces of conversation. Time becomes immaterial and associative memories fail -- is this a washing machine or a dryer? -- and day to day functioning becomes difficult.

According to the Global Deterioration Scale, also known as the Reisberg Scale, Alzheimer's progresses as follows:

[Stage 1 – No impairment. Memory and cognitive abilities appear normal.

Stage 2 – Minimal Impairment/Normal Forgetfulness. Memory lapses and changes in thinking are rarely detected by friends, family, or medical personnel, especially as about half of all people over 65 begin noticing problems in concentration and word recall.

Stage 3 – Early Confusional/Mild Cognitive Impairment. While subtle difficulties begin to impact function, the person may consciously or subconsciously try to cover up his or her problems. Expect to experience difficulty with retrieving words, planning, organization, misplacing objects, and forgetting recent learning, which can affect life at home and work. Depression and other changes in mood can also occur. Duration: 2 to 7 years.

Stage 4 – Late Confusional/Mild Alzheimer's. Problems handling finances result from mathematical challenges. Recent events and conversations are increasingly forgotten, although most people in this stage still know themselves and their family. Experience problems carrying out sequential tasks, including cooking, driving, ordering food at restaurants, and shopping. Often withdraw from social situations, become defensive, and deny problems. Accurate diagnosis of Alzheimer's disease is possible at this stage. Lasts roughly 2 years.

Stage 5 – Early Dementia/Moderate Alzheimer's disease. Decline is more severe and requires assistance. No longer able to manage independently or unable to recall personal history details and contact information. Frequently disoriented regarding place and or time. People in this stage experience a severe decline in numerical abilities and judgment skills, which can leave them vulnerable to scams and at risk from safety issues. Basic daily living tasks like feeding and dressing require increased supervision. Duration: an average of 1.5 years.

Stage 6 – Middle Dementia/Moderately Severe Alzheimer's disease. Total lack of awareness of present events and inability to accurately remember the past. People in this stage progressively lose the ability to take care of daily living activities like dressing, using the toilet and eating but are still able to respond to nonverbal stimuli, and communicate pleasure and pain via behavior. Agitation and hallucinations often show up in the late afternoon or evening. Dramatic personality changes such as wandering or suspicion of family members are common. Many can't remember close family members, but know they are familiar. Lasts approximately 2.5 years.

Stage 7 – Late or Severe Dementia and Failure to Thrive. In this final stage, speech becomes severely limited, as well as the ability to walk or sit. Total support around the clock is needed for all functions of daily living and care. Duration is impacted by quality of care and average length is 1 to 2.5 years.]

I find this list misleading and woefully short of detail, and it's an example of why I find it so hard to trust the medical community's advice and counsel for the identification and treatment of Alzheimer's. The list is virtually pointless, because any given symptom from one stage can and will show up in another stage. Moreover, in the big picture, what does it matter what stage a person is in?

In my opinion, if you want accurate, up to date knowledge of what can and can't be accomplished, you need to talk to the people who, minute by minute, hour by hour, and day by day, are living with the Alzheimer's sufferer. They are the people who can tell you what to do and how best to respond to an Alzheimer's sufferer's needs. Unfortunately, even with issues unrelated to diagnosis and treatment, the medical establishment operates on the basis of a hierarchy, and in this hierarchy the M.D. is top dog.

Don't misunderstand. Your loved one's doctor is a critical part of the health care process, but it's also a source of potential problems. You bring your loved one to the doctor or the doctor makes a house call and the visit takes all of fifteen minutes, if that. A normal person can be examined and diagnosed in fifteen minutes, because he or she can communicate with the doctor in a rational manner. An Alzheimer's sufferer can't. He or she can't tell a doctor what's wrong, what hurts. In later stages of the disease, they don't even know what's happening to them. For all they know they're being tortured by a group of strangers. They might not even know they're being attended to medically. For example -- and I can tell you this with absolute confidence -- a gynecological exam on a woman with severe Alzheimer's disease is tantamount to a rape.

About a year before my mother died, she had command of perhaps ten words and she could maybe put three or four together in a sentence. About six months before she died, she could only say single words. Yes. No. Good. Please. Help. The last three months of her life she could only utter sounds, if anything at all. During this intermediate period, in the last six months of her life, she developed what seemed to be a chronic gynecological condition. I say "seemed" because it was never diagnosed satisfactorily. The doctors couldn't figure out what it was and the treatments weren't working. I finally had to tell the doctors: "That's it! No More! Give her something for the pain. Whatever it takes."

When family members are upset because their loved one is in pain or major discomfort, doctors and caregivers feel the pressure to find a solution. But primary caregivers are reluctant to speak up. In fact, any self-respecting resident care facility or nursing home will make sure the nurses and aids keep their opinions to themselves. If you want to know what nurses and aids think, you have to pry it out of them. Consequently, it behooves you to spend the time to establish relationships with these people. If they trust you, they will talk to you. They will tell you what drugs work and which ones don't. They will tell you how long the doctor spends with your loved one during a routine visit and if they think the proposed treatment is worth pursuing. I can't tell you how many times I heard the doctor or the physicians assistant talk about a drug treatment plan that sounded like a Let's-Throw-This-At-It-And-See-If-It-Sticks plan.

Do I have a better plan? Is there some secret solution for end of life care that supersedes all other solutions? Hardly. All I can say is the following:

The best you can do for a loved one who has Alzheimer's is stay close to them and pay attention. Do not make decisions based on what you would want for yourself, or what somebody else thinks is best for them according to standards established for people with healthy brains.

28. What is the Right Thing to Do?

Despite the falls and the time I found her in such a terrible state on the bed, I liked the place we chose. The staff were kind and attentive, and my mother was always clean and dressed in fresh clothes. Her bed was neat and tidy; her sheets and linens always smelled fresh. The place never had a bad odor, and maintenance and physical updates seemed to be done on a regular schedule. The kitchen did a respectable job on meals, and there were always snacks available, from cookies and cakes to fresh fruit and yogurt.

This is not to say I didn't find faults. On the contrary, I had to continually remind the staff that my mother was lactose intolerant. It drove me crazy to come in and find my mother sitting over an ice cream sundae. It took a year but I think I finally got it through their thick heads not to serve my mom a glass of milk with dinner. When she made the move originally, and I filled out the dietary part of the application, I explicitly mentioned her lactose intolerance and her aversion to certain uncooked vegetables. And yet, for whatever reason, this information continually got waylaid somewhere between management and the front line. It was either for this reason, or because staff-resident interactions form a natural bond that on occasion detour established institutional guidelines.

For example:

The staff exist to please all of their residents. They are there to make the last years of a person's life as comfortable and as enjoyable as possible. So when all the residents but one are seated around the kitchen table eating big, fat chocolate sundaes, it's hard, if not impossible, to tell that one lactose-intolerant person they can't have one, too. Again, a person with Alzheimer's won't see this as a protective measure.

You can talk to them at length, ad nauseam, about lactose intolerance. It won't make a difference. To them, you're simply excluding them from a group activity and denying them something they want. It's a form of torture.

A doctor or dietician would come in and simply say, "She can't have dairy. Period! It will cause her a lot of discomfort and annoyance."

But which is worse? Isn't it equally bad to have an Alzheimer's sufferer denied something everyone else is enjoying?

Sure, there are alternatives. And this is where most resident care facilities fall short. They don't adapt and improvise as well as they could. They don't do that great a job of individuating care. That's where you come in. You have to say, "I found this nondairy ice cream, and I'm willing to provide it for my mother."

In my mother's case, when I finally said this, the facility went and bought the nondairy substitute on their own and made it available.

Resident care isn't perfect. And while the tendency for someone in private pay is to say, "Wait a minute, I'm paying for this. I should get it the way I want," it's equally important to remember that what you want is not necessarily what your loved would want, not, necessarily, at this stage in their life. You might think you're the best person to determine what your mother and father would want, but I would argue that the people who are closest to your loved one now, the staff and PCAs who are taking care of them day in and day out, also need to be considered and consulted, more so even than your loved one's doctors and closest friends.

This is why it's so important to maintain an almost intimate connection to the staff. Let's say you've filled out the dietary guidelines for your father or mother and for whatever reason they're not being followed. Suddenly the staff and the nurse are seeing chronic abdominal discomfort and bloating. They call in the doctor and the doctor spends fifteen minutes with your father or mother. They have no basis from which to make a proper diagnosis. They can't feel anything with their hands and they can't get any meaningful information directly from the patient. So they call for a CAT scan or MRI.

Thank heavens you're there to hit the stop and think button. You and you alone can avoid a lot of unnecessary diagnostics, not to mention the added discomfort, confusion, fear and costs.

So, among the many other things of which you have to be aware, you also want to make sure the dietary guidelines you've set down from the start are being adhered to.

Another reason to stay connected to the staff is so you'll be aware of the subtle changes in your loved one's health. I have to admit, this one got away from me.

My mother left her home in Maine with the ability to communicate. She could walk over two miles on her own, and she could dress herself and take care of all her own hygienic requirements. She left because she could not manage her time or her medications, occasionally forgot to bathe, could not cook for herself or do laundry, was unhappy with the tedium and boredom of normal life and would not or could not sit still for more than fifteen minutes at a time.

After seven months at the home, and after being on Seroquel for three months, she could still communicate, still walk, still enjoy the things that made her happy. We still talked about things we could see, touch, hear and taste. And her weight was only slightly more than it was when she left Maine.

By July of 2008, a year later, she had gained 60 pounds, was incontinent, and needed a walker to get around. She still recognized me but couldn't recognize her sister. When my brother came to visit in August, she went in and out of knowing who he was. At the same time, she was very, very happy and contented. She took part in activities and would still communicate her needs. She could talk to a nurse and a doctor and tell them what hurt or what felt wrong, and she and I could still speak to each other about things we could touch, hear, taste and smell, although it wasn't nearly what it was a year earlier. She still took Seroquel.

A few months later, sometime during that fall or early winter of 2008, she would have that extremely disturbing incontinence episode in her room. After this episode, things would change quickly and dramatically. By June of 2009 she would be catatonic and unable to communicate. She would be unable to feed herself without prompting, and eventually reach a point where she couldn't eat without someone feeding her.

Did she have a stroke that made her catatonic and unable to feed herself? I don't know. It seems likely. If she had a stroke, why didn't someone inform me? The staff? Management? Her doctor? Why didn't I notice? I was still going to see her once and sometimes more often per week.

When I think back, I can't remember a sudden, distinct change. I can't remember it being one way one day and a different way the next. I remember a slow and steady degradation of function, many visits of just sitting next to her or lying next to her. I remember her inability to communicate anything more than a few words. And then I remember one of the staff telling me my mom needed to move to a different health care environment, that she wasn't eating and they, the staff, weren't allowed to feed her. Not long after I remember getting a telephone call from management saying the time had come for her to move to a nursing home. I remember a process of looking for the right bed in the right place and spending about three weeks doing it. But three whole months had gone by between the time she should have been admitted to a nursing home and the time she left for a full care facility. In those three months she lost the sixty pounds she had gained on Seroquel.

Seroquel almost certainly caused her weight gain, and it may very well have been responsible for the stroke that caused her catatonic stupor. On the other hand, the added weight provided the cushion she needed to survive the aftermath of the event and her catatonia. Had she been her old weight when she had the stroke, it's possible she never would have lived through the three months of weight loss.

I have more than a little bit of skepticism about the way the residential care facility handled this stage of my mother's care. Were they just watching her fade away? Were they not feeding her at all? Were they putting a plate in front of her at the dinner table, waiting for everyone to eat and finish eating, and then just taking all the dirty plates away including the full plate in front of my mother? The answer to this last question is, yes? For a while they were. Until two members of the staff took it upon himself to feed my mother, against the institution's protocols and policy mind you, this is exactly what was happening.

This is another reason why it's better to find a place that can provide assisted living and continuing care in the same physical location, because, in addition to making the transition from one to the other easier and less traumatic for the resident, it offers an extra measure of professional care just beyond the next door.

But here's the kicker: While I feel I waited too long to move my mother into full time nursing care, and feel there may have been a link between Seroquel and her stroke, and that perhaps the facility did not react quickly enough to her needs, the fact remains that when I finally moved her to a nursing home a few miles away, it was clear from her reaction that she would have rather stayed where she was.

29. The Broken Promise

September 9, 2009, was the day I officially broke my promise to my mother. I swore I would never place her in a nursing home, but at around 11:30 in the morning on September 9, on a beautiful, bright, sunny late summer New England day, she was transported by ambulance to a continuing care and rehabilitation facility in Concord, New Hampshire to live out the last two years, one month and eleven days of her life.

I wanted to be there to escort her to her new home. Unfortunately, at the last minute, the ambulance service and the resident care director changed their plans. They bumped-up the pickup time. I was still three-and-one-half hours away and couldn't get there until thirty minutes or so after she was due to be walked through the doors of the nursing home. As you would expect, I was a little peeved they couldn't accommodate my schedule or stick to the original plan. Fortunately, one of the staff members, G[7], from the resident care facility, offered to ride along in the ambulance. G also said he would sit with my mom until I got there. This was the same guy who had taken such good care of her the last two years and the same guy who had been feeding her the last three months.

I arrived at the nursing home at about noon. My mother was on the third floor with G. The two of them sat at a round table in the middle of the dining room, really just a regular room with a big screen TV and half a dozen large

---

[7] G. was one of the most caring and considerate PCAs at the resident care facility. He worked tirelessly, effortlessly and selflessly. He's a credit to his vocation. There are others, of course, and I will only single them out by their first initials. D. S. A. and J.

tables. G was feeding her, or trying to. About twenty or more other residents were also dining. These people were in various stages of end of life care. A few were very old and very sick. Mutterings and moaning could be heard from almost every corner of the home.

I walked to my mother and gave her a kiss. She wouldn't look at me. She wouldn't eat her food. G was being very patient.

Clearly she knew the difference between where she had been and where she was now. To her, she had been taken from her home and dropped off at a nursing home to die. I had thought, maybe, in her catatonic state, she wouldn't know the difference. I was wrong. She knew. She knew me. She knew where she was. And she didn't like it.

She was crying. There was no sound. Just a few tears.

It was about all I could stand.

I thanked G and asked if she had eaten anything. He just shook his head.

I had some people to see and papers to sign and told G I would be back in a few minutes. He said he would wait until I returned. God bless him. I took the elevator downstairs and completed the required paperwork. I spent a few minutes with the management staff, whom I'd met two weeks earlier, signed a check and confirmed that my mother's DNR order and living will were on file. I also made sure the facility had all the necessary contact numbers, then I went back upstairs and relieved G.

My mother and I sat in the dining room next to each other. I tried to feed her but she wouldn't eat. She wouldn't even look at me. It was heartbreaking.

One of the nurses came over and asked if she could help. I nodded and gave her my seat. She sat with my mom, tried to touch her hair, but my mom flinched a little. The nurse relented and said, "That's OK, Judy. I'm sorry." The nurse's voice was gentle and compassionate. She said to me, "We'll take care of her. Why don't you get some lunch and come back?"

This nurse, we'll call her A, turned out to be an angel in disguise.

I kissed my mother goodbye and told her I would see her in an hour. She didn't acknowledge me. I thought to myself, "What have I done? And what's her first night going to be like?"

Not only did I break my promise about placing her in a nursing home, I had her going into a double room because a private room hadn't been available. And her roommate, a woman in her mid-sixties crippled by MD and completely non-ambulatory, could barely move her head or any other part of her body; her feet, legs and forearms were twisted and bent at painful angles.

At the time my intention was to move my mother into a private room when one became available. But as it turned out, the double room, which she shared with this non-ambulatory person who happened to love country music and old movies, turned out to be the best of all possible arrangements.

When making decisions for someone who can't make decisions for themselves, we tend to see everything in terms of what we would want for ourselves. Or maybe, we think we know what someone might want based on what we knew of the person when they were young and strong and fiercely independent. But that was then. "Now" conjures up a whole new set of rules and guidelines. Forty years ago my mother would not have wanted a roommate. Then again, forty years ago my mother wasn't afraid of being alone.

I left the nursing home and booked a room at the Days Inn down the road. I planned to stay in Concord so that I'd be readily available through the transition period. At the time, little did I know the extent to which the staff[8] would reach out and care for my mother. I had no idea they would be warm and affectionate, not just with her but with everyone. They weren't afraid to touch, caress and even kiss residents on the cheek or forehead. Over the next two years, while spending time at this particular nursing home, I would learn to express warmth and caring in similar ways. For example, it was common practice at the nursing home to get in very close to a resident when talking to them, in some cases, close enough for you and the resident to be touching foreheads.

This brings up another interesting conundrum regarding the decision making process. When choosing a nursing home (or a hospital) how much importance do you place on reviews, reports and regulatory agency statistics? Clearly, if you read that a particular nursing home has accrued multiple abuse violations over the course of a few years,

---

[8] I can't say enough about the staff at this nursing home. For the most part, they became my mother's end of life family.

it's one thing. These kinds of violations speak of inappropriate staffing and substandard management. But what about other code violations? Would you stay away from a nursing home if you saw a chart that showed the home had open and unresolved fire safety violations?

My experience is that you can't trust reports based solely on statistics.

One day I walked into the home and noticed for the first time that every resident had on a hospital style I.D. bracelet. When I asked the nurse about it she said they had to put them on the residents because the fire safety inspector came in and wrote them up for a safety violation. He also wrote them up for keeping doors open and not keeping a pathway to the elevator.

I hated those bracelets, and so did the residents. And while keeping the doors closed may indeed prevent a fire from spreading through the halls, it's no way to live or run a nursing home. The residents can't open and close doors themselves.

Many years ago, when I was a young man, I worked at a summer camp. I loved the camp. Why? Because there was much warmth, camaraderie and companionship between the campers and counselors. Nobody was afraid of a hug or a kiss on the cheek. It wasn't uncommon for girl counselors and their campers to sleep in a big huddle on the floor during thunder and lightning storms. Boys and girls used to go camping in a big teepee that could accommodate thirty or more people.

That was in the sixtes and early seventies. By the eighties, things had changed. Someplace in the U.S. a little girl of ten came home and told mommy and daddy her counselor slept with her during a bad thunder storm. The parents sued and won, and perfectly innocent and caring behavior became off-limits. So now, because there are parents everywhere who choose to live in abject fear, kids in summer camp have to make it through the night all on their own.

The point I'm trying to make is that you can't just read the reports and the reviews and then make a decision. You have to look at the place from the inside. Does it smell? How long have the staff been there? Look at the bulletin board. Does it seem like a friendly, open place? Are you at liberty to walk anywhere you want? Is the kitchen clean? How's the food?

If the average employment period for a nurse, PCA, groundskeeper, maintenance man and kitchen person is over 4 years, that's good. If there's a PCA or nurse who has been working at the place for fifteen years, even better. But if the turnover is every four months to a year, then the place has a problem.

What about the residents themselves? How old is the oldest? How many years have the veteran residents been there?

Obviously, these rules aren't inalterable. There are always exceptions. But it's a good place to start. In my case, I had word of mouth recommendations. I had been told good things about the facility by the PCAs and nurses who worked at the resident care facility from which my mother had just been transferred. I had walked through the home and talked to the staff. There were PCAs who had been working there for more than fifteen years. The oldest resident was also the oldest living person in New England, and she had been a resident for 11 years. There were other residents at the home who had been there many years. It wasn't fancy or posh. The rooms were small. But it had something, something special. And if I had to describe it with one word I would say it had "spunkiness."

In other words, strict compliance to the established rules of institutional guardianship took a back seat to a performance criteria that made the facility more of a home, a real home.

After all, it's a place for people to live out their lives. Not a prison.

30. Adjusting to the New Home

My mother wasn't happy on Day-Two, nor was she at Day-Three. And every hour that passed I kept thinking to myself, well, if it doesn't work out, I'll just take her home and do the best I can. Staring at the ceiling in my motel room, I would ask myself, is this it? Is this the best we can hope for? Is this what's in store for me, for all of us if we're lucky? Then, on the fourth day, something changed. If I had to guess what it was, I would say she came to understand that the PCAs and nurses at the facility were caring for her in the same way her mother cared for her when she was just a little kid. I doubt she realized this through cognition. It was just something she felt viscerally.

By the end of the first week the staff had my mother up and walking again. By the end of the second week she was talking, smiling and even laughing. She occasionally blew kisses at some of the nurses and her primary caregivers. She was eating well, exercising and sleeping well. Was she happy? I doubt it. But she was comfortable and clean. She seemed OK.

I went home, paid bills and conducted some business. I took three days. I mowed the lawns, prepared for winter, and then I reversed course and headed back to Concord.

Mom seemed to have adjusted. But it wasn't like the adjustment she had made to the resident care facility. In resident care, she was at home. In nursing care, she was at A Home. Somehow she knew the difference.

One weekend Sandra and I went to Concord together. We took my mother outside for a walk. It was a beautiful fall day, warm and sunny. We sat on the patio for a while. Sandra and I tried to make conversation. We got little in response. A word here or there. "Pretty. Nice. Yes. No. Good. Warm. Cold." About what she was capable of before her stroke-like episode at the resident care facility.

After about thirty minutes of sitting I decided to take her for a stroll. We walked around the parking lot, she in the wheelchair, me pushing, Sandra on our left. We spun around the lot and then headed for the street. Sandra started talking about how beautiful the day was, and how everyone was gearing-up for the holidays. She said something to the effect: "The big turkey dinner with all the fixin's is right around the corner." At this point we were at the end of the parking lot starting down the street.

Suddenly, while Sandra was saying something about Christmas and Chanukah being here before too long, and while we had turned the corner to head down the street, my mother said, "Stop, it's too painful."

Sandra and I looked at each other. I leaned toward my mom and asked, "What? What hurts, Ma? Do you want to head back? Are you cold? Is it too bumpy?"

But it was gone. Whatever she was talking about. The cold. The road. Leaving the comfort and security of the home. The Holidays. To this day -- and I think about it a lot -- I have no idea what was, "Too painful."

It troubles me beyond description to think my mother had just enough of her memory intact to realize a celebration of The Holidays would be way too painful to tolerate.

"Stop, it's too painful," was the last full sentence my mother would ever say to me.

31. Shift Change

Every day I visited my mom she would be dressed and up and around. She rarely stayed in bed, unless she had the flu, which happened only once. Of course, toward the end, during the last six months of her life, she clocked considerably more bed time for obvious reasons.

There was one time, however, I had to raise an alarm. It was the time I found her in bed on the verge of heat stroke.

It was summer. Hot. I got to the third floor, said hello to everyone and noticed the nurse on duty. She was someone I hadn't yet the pleasure of meeting. I asked the whereabouts of my mom but nobody really knew. Someone said, "She must be in her room."

I found her in her room all right, in bed. She was sweaty and unresponsive. I immediately went back to the front desk and told the nurse. I calmly informed her my mother wasn't doing well and that she was sweating and unresponsive. I could tell this nurse didn't think I knew very much and didn't like being interrupted. I said, "It's almost as if she's had a stroke."

When she heard me say the word, "Stroke," the nurse rolled her eyes. I didn't cop an attitude or say anything else as we walked down the hall to my mom's room. I knew the situation would do all the talking for me.

The nurse sat on the bed and checked my mother. She shined a light into her eyes. She said, "Hmm."

She took her pulse. She said, "Hmm," again. Then she felt my mother's back.

"You're right," she said. "Her pulse is high. I think she's overheated."

The nurse left briefly to retrieve a cold washcloth and a glass of water. She came back, elevated my mother and began dabbing her with the washcloth. She got her to drink some water. She talked to her, calling her by her first name, and worked quickly and efficiently. Within minutes my mother was smiling and drinking on her own from the glass. In another fifteen minutes she would be dressed and watching TV with me as if nothing had happened.

To this day, I wonder what would have happened if she had indeed suffered a life-threatening stroke. Is it possible she might have avoided the terrible agony and discomfort that would befall her later? Of course, there was never a choice. What else was I to do? Wait outside her door until she had succumbed to heat stroke? That would have been absurd. What I did, what the nurse managed to do, was a simple metabolic correction, not to be confused with the words "extraordinary measures" frequently used in a standard DNR.

I never blamed this nurse or anyone else at the home for what happened that day, and, in time, I learned to trust and respect the nurse. However, I made a note to myself to vary the timing of my visits as much as possible. In particular, I made a note to be around more often during normal staff rotations.

The fact is, nobody placed my mother in a bed with too many covers, on a hot day, with little or nothing to drink, intending to cause heat stroke. It just happened, inadvertently. And it happened because of something that occurs in every hospital, resident care facility, nursing home, rehab clinic, laboratory, mental health facility, you name it, all over the world. It's called: Shift Change.

After breakfast that morning, my mother was probably cold and tired. The morning PCA asked the morning nurse what to do and the nurse suggested putting her back in bed for a while. So Mom went back to bed. And she got covered up warm and cozy because it was still morning and still on the chilly side. Temperatures, even inside, were cool in the morning, but as the day wore on, the facility's climate control system struggled to catch up to correct for the staggering afternoon heat on a midsummer's day. As time passed, the temperature rose. The morning PCA got ready to leave around 2:30 in the afternoon, or maybe for some reason had to leave early, and her 3:00 PM replacement hadn't arrived yet. There's your thirty minute window of opportunity for something to happen.

Meanwhile, as frustrating and unfortunate as this episode was at the time, it paled in comparison to what happened months later, when her insurance company, her pharmacy and her doctor took her off of her blood pressure medicine of thirty years. Suffice it to say that one event is a matter of circumstance while the other represents a complete failure of the medical system.

32. The Failure of Modern Medicine

Let me count the ways.

First, we all know the woefully insufficient means by which modern medicine treats Alzheimer's and dementia and many other diseases. At best, it's a one-armed man filling sand bags to stem the flood of a tsunami. And government, corporations and insurance companies have way too much control over the management of your health. It's a given. We all know it.

But where the thing gets really ugly is at the pharmacy.

My mother had been on the same blood pressure medicine at the same dosages for thirty years. Norvasc and Toprol. She took 10 mg of the former and 150 mg of the latter, and over the years these two medicines, at these dosages, did a good job of maintaining her blood pressure at a reasonable 130 over 80-something.

Enter her secondary insurance company, AARP and the Medicare Pharmacy Program.

Somewhere along the line I got a letter from AARP telling me that Toprol would no longer be available as a copay option. Remember, AARP only paid about $6.00 a month toward this drug. I was paying out of pocket about $86.00. But it was a good drug. It worked. And my mom had been on it a long, long, long time.

I ignored the letter. Why should I care? Screw AARP and Medicare because I was paying out of pocket for the drug anyway. Did they really think I would need to make a change for $72 a year? Boy, did I have another thing coming.

Turned out, the letter I received also went to the pharmacy and my mother's doctor. And without my permission or my mother's permission or anybody else's permission, the pharmacy, the doctor and the insurance company decided on their own to discontinue the drug's use. If it hadn't been for Nurse A at the home calling to tell me that Toprol was no longer on my mother's schedule I would have never known.

Naturally, I was steamed. I contacted the pharmacy first and demanded to know why they had done this. They told me the insurance company was no longer paying for it. I said, "Who the hell cares? They weren't paying for it to start with."

The pharmacy told me the doctor approved the change. So I called the doctor. I spoke with her and she claimed my mother didn't need the drug anymore. I said, "First of all, I'm in charge. Not you. Second, who stops a drug cold turkey? She's been on this for thirty years. Scale it back and see how she responds."

Which is what we decided to do.

But think about it. The doctor didn't initiate this change. She didn't suddenly look at my mother's chart or examine her and say to herself: "Hmm, looks like we can start to scale back on her blood pressure meds." Instead, she got a letter from the insurance company telling her to find a suitable, generic replacement or consider not using the drug at all. Then she looked at the chart.

Let me tell you something about charts. They can mess you up.

So we scaled back on the drug and my mother responded poorly. She did a good deal of sweating. Cold sweating. Naturally, we bumped her back up a little to control the sweating. Eventually she would get off all her drugs, but that's another part of the story.

33. Countdown to Defeat

If ever I felt like calling a lawyer and screaming the word "lawsuit" it was when I found out the insurance company had taken my mother off Toprol. But a lot was going on with my mother's health at this time. Strange, unforeseen things were happening. The doctor was stumped. The nurses and staff were desperate to find my mother some relief. Nothing worked. Nothing helped. She was agitated, uncomfortable, in pain, and nobody could tell me why.

The first time I noticed the problem was when we were headed downstairs to a concert in the main dining room. I had wheeled my mother to the elevator and before we got there she had an intense episode of scratching, almost like a spasm. She had no control over it. I asked the nurse if she was aware of it and she said my mother just started doing it the day before. The nurse added she had already called the doctor because she suspected the cause of the spasm was vaginitis.

I took my mother to the concert but had to bring her back upstairs because it was too humiliating for her to be in public. I felt so badly for her. She couldn't stop herself. Every two or three minutes she would attack her genital area in a fit of intense scratching.

This condition, in one form or another, would get much worse. It would haunt my mother until two weeks before her death. In addition, she had begun tensing her jaw and violently grinding her teeth. At times, I could cup her chin in my hand and gently massage her cheeks and say, "Ma, smile. Give us a big smile and relax your jaw." I would laugh and try to make a joke out of it. This worked for a while, a month or two, and then the effort made the situation worse. I hate to admit it, but it was difficult to be close to her while she was grinding her teeth. It was like having someone scraping a chalk board with their fingernails. Only in this case, it wasn't just an irritation, it was a serious health concern. How long could she go on doing it before breaking off the tops of all her molars?

As promised, the nurse at the home arranged for the doctor to see my mom a day or two later. The doctor conducted a genital exam and figured my mother had a vaginal infection, but the diagnosis wasn't really conclusive. Both her blood test and the culture came back negative. Was the redness and irritation the cause of the itching, or was it the other way around? They couldn't say for sure. Regardless, they started her on a prescription cream in the hope of reducing some of the irritation and redness.

This condition persisted for a month. And then it got worse. The cream didn't work; neither did a prescription dose of antibiotics. Every week, one of the doctors or a Physician's Assistant was back for another round of invasive, humiliating poking and prodding. Finally, I was at wits' end. I had to tell the doctors and the PA to give it a rest. If they couldn't find the cause after all the exams they had already conducted, they weren't going to find it. They had to stop torturing my mother.

I remember one terrible visit. My mother was in obvious agony. I sat with her outside her room for two hours. She was in a new chair that afforded her a great deal more security and comfort than the old one. I sat next to her and massaged her hand and rubbed her forehead and just tried to say soothing things to her to get her to stop shaking and twitching. The muscles in her arms and hands would get taught and tense. Her tendons and ligaments would feel like gnarled rope. She didn't seem to be scratching anymore. It was more like a spasm. Uncontrollable and very painful.

Sometimes she would make a tremulous sound when the spasm would get hold of her, as if she were being shaken from within. And she would look at me with pleading eyes. It even happened to her when she tried to sleep. She would close her eyes and be quiet for a minute or two and then abruptly she would open her eyes and stare into space and the spasm would take control. It seemed to me she could only sleep off and on for minutes at a time.

I called the doctor's office. I told the receptionist I didn't want to speak to the PA. My mother's original doctor wasn't in so the receptionist put me on the phone with the new resident. Apparently, unbeknownst to me, my mother had become this resident's patient. The resident, a young woman fresh out of medical school, said she had seen my mother just a few days earlier. She added that my mother didn't have any infection, that her genital area looked normal, and that she seemed to be in good shape and not in any pain.

I flipped. I said, "Wait a minute. How long were you with her?"

The resident said, "I guess about ten minutes."

It was probably more like five minutes.

I said, "Well, I was just sitting with her for two hours and I'm telling you, she's in pain. If you were with her for more than a few minutes you would know this."

I could hear pages turning, and I knew she was looking at my mom's chart. The dreaded chart. A compilation of information gathered and stored for simultaneously making a diagnosis from afar and covering one's own ass.

"Forget the chart," I said. "Listen to what I'm saying. She's in pain, or intense discomfort. She grinds her teeth constantly. She has spasms. She has contracture."

"OK, I believe you," she said. "It's possible your mother has atrophic vaginitis. It's a thinning of the vaginal walls. Elderly women are very susceptible to this. This could be the cause of the itching."

"It's not an itch anymore," I said. "It's more than that."

"I don't know what that could be," she said. "It could be a consequence of her disease. Would you like me to have Doctor E.[9] call you?"

"Yes," I said. "Thank you."

---

[9] I'm calling her Doctor E. to avoid using names. For the record, I thought Doctor E. was a very competent doctor; one who made house calls and cared about her patients, which only goes to prove that even the best doctors have severe limitations. In addition, as good as Doctor E. was, her practice and her office's level of care suffered as her patient load increased. I believe this was the result of her turning her patients over to her new PA and resident.

34. Myoclonus

Doctor E. called me on my cell phone the following day. We spent twenty minutes or more talking about my mother. At first, weeks before, during an earlier conversation, she had said she didn't know the reason for my mother's intense spasms. She also admitted she had never seen this type of violent, uncontrollable scratching or spasming in an Alzheimer's sufferer before. This time she was playing a slightly different tune.

I had prepared myself for the conversation by doing as much background research as I could on disorders and diseases that cause muscle spasms. Almost nowhere on the Web could I find references to spasms, twitching or uncontrollable muscle movements, caused by Alzheimer's disease. There were a few references, but only as part of a larger list. On a Web page discussing Myoclonus, I found the following:

What is myoclonus?

Myoclonus describes a symptom and generally is not a diagnosis of a disease. It refers to sudden, involuntary jerking of a muscle or group of muscles. Myoclonic twitches or jerks usually are caused by sudden muscle contractions, called positive myoclonus, or by muscle relaxation, called negative myoclonus. Myoclonic jerks may occur alone or in sequence, in a pattern or without pattern. They may occur infrequently or many times each minute. Myoclonus sometimes occurs in response to an external event or when a person attempts to make a movement. The twitching cannot be controlled by the person experiencing it.

In its simplest form, myoclonus consists of a muscle twitch followed by relaxation. A hiccup is an example of this type of myoclonus. Other familiar examples of myoclonus are the jerks or "sleep starts" that some people experience while drifting off to sleep. These simple forms of myoclonus occur in normal, healthy persons and cause no difficulties. When more widespread, myoclonus may involve persistent, shock-like contractions in a group of muscles. In some cases, myoclonus begins in one region of the body and spreads to muscles in other areas. More severe cases of myoclonus can distort movement and severely limit a person's ability to eat, talk, or walk. These types of myoclonus may indicate an underlying disorder in the brain or nerves.

What are the causes of myoclonus?

Myoclonus may develop in response to infection, head or spinal cord injury, stroke, brain tumors, kidney or liver failure, lipid storage disease, chemical or drug poisoning, or other disorders. Prolonged oxygen deprivation to the brain, called hypoxia, may result in posthypoxic myoclonus. Myoclonus can occur by itself, but most often it is one of several symptoms associated with a wide variety of nervous system disorders. For example, myoclonic jerking may develop in patients with multiple sclerosis, Parkinson's disease, Alzheimer's disease, or Creutzfeldt-Jakob disease. Myoclonic jerks commonly occur in persons with epilepsy, a disorder in which the electrical activity in the brain becomes disordered leading to seizures.[10]

Naturally, when the doctor called, I wanted to know if my mother was suffering symptoms from some other disease. Did she have Parkinson's, Tourette's, Huntington's,

---

[10] From HealingWell.com

Wilson's, Fibromyalgia, Epilepsy, Tardive Dystonia, ALS, etc.?

One by one the doctor refuted the diseases, ruling them out by virtue of the attributable symptoms my mother didn't have, or the fact that she didn't posses the proper genetic markers.

"So it's the Alzheimer's," I said. "Pure and simple."

"Most likely," she said.

"And the fact her spasms are almost identical to the movement she was making when she had the violent scratching attacks?"

"It could be muscle memory. Or maybe the brain pathways she used when she had the infection are the only ones still functioning. It's hard to say. Clearly, though, what's happening to your Mom is a consequence of the natural progression of the disease."

Seroquel?

"Is there anything we can do?" I said.

"We can try anti-seizure meds and pain killers."

"Yes," I said. "Let's do that. There's no reason for her to have to suffer. She shouldn't be suffering. It's not right."

"I agree," she said. "It's not right. Let's try to make her more comfortable."

"Yes, thank you. And let's not bother with any more exams. There's no point to it anymore."

"OK, we can do that."

And so another milestone was reached. From this day forward, her care would be palliative.

I don't know why but after I hung up with the doctor I thought back to a visit that took place a month or so earlier. The nurse had called in a dentist to take a look at a bad tooth in the front left side of my mother's mouth. His recommendation was to drill it and put in a temporary filling. He had called me to talk about the pros and cons. He said if the cavity enlarged and encompassed the other teeth and her gum, her mouth might bleed and start to hurt and she might have trouble eating. She could also break a tooth and swallow it accidentally. How long would it take for all this to happen? Maybe a year. Maybe less. Did she have a year? Was it worth putting her through this procedure? Yes, if she lived a year. No, if she lived six months. What a horrible way to have to decide somebody's care.

Following a short deliberation I decided to go ahead with the work. The dentist said he could do the whole thing at her bedside in the home and that it would only take fifteen minutes. He assured me that if it looked like my mother was not going to sit still or open her mouth then we would just cancel the procedure. I figured, great, if my mother doesn't want it done, she'll just keep her mouth closed.

I met the dentist at the home on the day of the procedure. I asked him if he would give her Novocain? He said it was up to me, but that people at my mother's age and level of dementia usually didn't have any nerve pain in their mouth. He added that if she were to flinch while he was giving her the injection, the needle could break and/or go askew. Decision made. No Novocain.

The nurse elevated my mom and laid a hand on her forehead. She talked to her and gave her a kiss and a hug. My mom smiled. I lovingly pinched her cheek and stood back to let the dentist get in close. My mother opened her mouth and he drilled the tooth with a handheld drill. She flinched a little. The gum bled. The whole time she was looking straight at me.

I have that picture of her in my head now, staring at me, flinching a little, her gum bleeding a little. I can't imagine what she was thinking at the time. Was she thinking anything at all? Did she know me? Did she know what was happening? She looked so helpless, so confused and afraid.

If I could, I would go back in time and change that memory.

35. Morphine

In June of 2011 my visits took a distinctive turn for the worst. My mother had almost continual spasms at this point, and it seemed to me they were aggravated by stress and anxiety. Moreover, her stress seemed to increase in proportion to my proximity, which meant I could no longer sit with her or take her anywhere. For the next six months, roughly, I would spend my visits with other residents or watch my mom from outside whatever room she happened to be in. Sometimes I would kiss her hello. Other times I would stay an hour, leave, then come back and try again.

The doctors and I were now trying to relieve her agitation and muscle spasms with drugs. It was a guessing game. How much is enough to relieve her symptoms but not enough to knock her out and prevent her from eating?

I suggested Tramadol. The P.A. suggested Lyrica. Both were tried, individually and together, and both failed to do the required job. The spasms continued. We tried varying dosages of both for about a month. In the end, we kept up with the Tramidol therapy and abandoned the Lyrica altogether. Lyrica would upset her stomach and I believe it probably gave her an intestinal bleed. Eventually, we would also stop the Tramidol, which might have made the spasms worse after apparently making them better. I know it sounds strange for one drug to solve the problem and then come right around and make the problem worse but it's how it works sometimes. An Alzheimer's patient might respond to a given drug based on nothing more than the change it puts them through. Later, as the drug builds in their system, and the change it created now becomes the status quo, the person backslides and responds to what the drug is doing metabolically and neurologically.

Meanwhile, along with the painful spasms and the grinding of her teeth, my mother was suffering from contracture. This happens for many different reasons, but in a person with advanced Alzheimer's it occurs when the brain no longer sends signals to the nerves and muscles. Muscles and tendons contract and stay that way. They become permanently shortened and can't be massaged or nursed back to health. Contracture in my mother had been going on for the better part of a year. She wore therapeutic hand supports to prevent her nails from digging into her palms.

In August I sidelined the Physician's Assistant and told her we had to do more. I wanted my mother to start low dose morphine therapy, sublingual. The doctor suggested Oxycodone. I couldn't believe it. I asked her why?

"We try to go with a less powerful drug if we can," she said.

"Forgive me but screw that," I said. "Have you seen my mother? Would you be suggesting Oxycodone if she was your mother?"

She relented, and finally, on morphine and Tramadol, my mother had some relief. The spasms were less pronounced, less violent. I can't say she was calm or comfortable but she was better. The nurses and PCAs thought so, too.

It was also about this time I called in hospice to help with palliative care. I did this because my mother's doctors were ill-equipped to do what needed to be done. They were drug shy and standoffish, which is a less kind way of saying they were diagnosis and treatment oriented.

I didn't have to wait long for hospice. They came the next day or the day after, met with my mother and me and did an evaluation. They started immediately, worked hand in hand with the PCAs and the nurses at the home, and spent quality time with my mother, feeding her, getting her to drink juice or water, reading to her, and, in the case of the hospice spiritual person, learned Hebrew so that he could read psalms to her in the way she had become accustomed to hearing them. The nursing home and its staff were still my mother's primary caregivers, and that was the way I wanted it.

On October 2 or 3, 2011, Nurse A called to tell me something had happened.

"Your Mom is different," she said. "She's more calm. Her hands aren't as tight and she doesn't have the twitch so much anymore. It's still there a little. Also, she isn't really eating. Only a little bit every day. Sometimes nothing at all."

"Do you think she had a stroke."

"Yes, if I had to guess. I think maybe she had a stroke. It's hard to say for sure."

When I got to Concord my mom was in bed. She was stable, calm and comfortable. At last, she seemed to have some peace.

36. The Last Two Weeks

On or about October 5 the duty nurse at the home informed me that my mom hadn't eaten anything all day. The entire week before, and even during the previous two weeks, she had been eating only minimally, just enough to survive. Now she was thin and frail and couldn't move any part of her body on her own. The staff had her on a two hour schedule for repositioning.

I drove to Concord and stayed the night. I went to her bedside and stroked her hair. She didn't really make eye contact, just stared at the wall. I had placed some pictures of her when she was young and some copies of photos of her family on that wall. I had tacked them in front of her, in her line of sight and close enough, I hoped, for her to see. I wanted the pictures to connect in some way, to spark recognition, if only for a moment.

In the back of my mind were comments First Lady Nancy Reagan had made to reporters and interviewers during and after her husband's battle with Alzheimer's. She had talked about Ronnie's soul not being affected by the disease and how she felt he was still in there, listening, connecting. I recall her saying that at the time of his final breath she felt he looked at her and there was a moment of recognition and love and understanding.

According to Keith Olberman of MSNBC News, Patti Davis, Ronald and Nancy Reagan's daughter, wrote an essay about her father's final few moments.

The exact quote from Ms, Davis, was "At the last moment when his breathing told us this was it, he opened his eyes and looked straight at my mother. Eyes that hadn't opened for days, did. And they weren't chalky or vague. They were clear, and blue, and full of love. If a death can be lovely, his was."

From what else his daughter wrote, the moment seemed to be described as a liberation for Nancy Reagan, too.

These words haunted me and had been haunting me for years. They are hopeful words to every person caring for a loved one with Alzheimer's. In the back of our minds, it's there, poking out, struggling to be accepted as a possibility. Hope. Unadulterated, pure . . . and full of desperation. In my case, a word, a look, a smile, anything to counteract the last full sentence she had spoken to me.

"Stop, it's too painful."

I spoke with the staff nurses and the hospice nurse. It was decided we would no longer try to feed her or give her anything but a saturated swab to drink. She couldn't swallow without the danger of choking. Her PCAs kept her clean and comfortable. They were kind and attentive. They repositioned her as needed, washed her daily, cleaned her mouth with a swab and moistened her lips and skin with moisturizers. I sat at her side and waited.

Every so often she would close her eyes. It would look, for a second or two, as if she were about to fall asleep. But then she would abruptly open her eyes with a start. I'd noticed this before. It had been going on for months. Sometimes it would happen while she was in her chair, sometimes while she was in bed. It was as if she were afraid to let herself fall asleep, as if she were afraid she wouldn't wake up.

I wondered if she had visions or hallucinations when her eyes were closed. I wondered if the morphine, or other drugs she had been taking over the last few years, caused her to have nightmares that made her afraid to sleep. I wondered if she were afraid to die.

She never had been afraid of much, although once I heard her say she was afraid of pain. I'm not sure from where exactly that sentiment came. After my father died she went to visit my brother. Coming out of a restaurant she slipped and broke her wrist. It didn't seem to slow her down much. Another time, before she had been diagnosed with Alzheimer's and a year or two before she had transferred into institutional care, she told me she wished she could take a pill that would end it all. Back then, she certainly wasn't afraid of death.

Afraid? I don't believe so. She was the woman who took a fishhook out of my eye, and once crushed a giant wasp in her bare hands. There was yet another time my friend's four year old son fell head first on the edge of the rock wall in the back of our house. My friend's wife became hysterical. My mother grabbed the kid, took him inside and made an ice pack for his head. She held him in her arms and soothed him. Quieted his mother, too.

I watched her kill snakes and rats in the yard, get rid of yellow jackets by pinching their nests off into plastic garbage bags. She had faced down wild dogs and other threats, travelled all over the world, flown in big and small planes, helicopters, been on safari, sailed the oceans in ships and small boats. She'd run rapids and climbed mountains. She had loved exotic foods and strange ports of call.

Why be afraid of death?

The hospice nurse came up to me and asked me if my mother was waiting for somebody. I said, no, I didn't think so. She asked if there was somebody else she needed to see before she passed. I said, no. My brother was here. He said his goodbyes a month ago. Moreover, he had wanted to come back out again, but I felt it wasn't necessary. For one thing, she wasn't really conscious. For another, he was going through his own trauma. His youngest son had just been diagnosed with a tumor on his brain stem.

"Have you told her it's OK?" the hospice nurse asked.

"Yes," I said.

"Have you talked to her about how you're OK with it?"

"Yes," I said. "In so many words. I tell her everything's all right. I tell her you're going to be in a wonderful place soon. You'll see Dad. And Joe and I are fine. We want you to be happy."

She nodded.

"Sometimes," she said, "People won't let themselves go if a loved one is in the room with them."

Right, like who could know that for sure? Has anyone ever come back from the dead and announced it? Has anyone on their death bed ever said it to anyone else by their bedside? I mean, other than Jason Robards at the end of Sergio Leoni's western tome, Once Upon a Time in the West, when he gets off his horse and he's gut shot and he sits down and tells Charles Bronson: "Go away. I don't want you to see me die." who the hell says something like that?

Nevertheless, she planted the seed. I had to think about it now.

I went out to lunch with a friend of mine who lived in the area. He asked me what was going on. I told him it was close. She was fighting. She didn't want to go. He said he was sorry and asked if there was anything he could do. A lot people asked that. They offer to help. It's comforting. People say things, sometimes, and they think they're helping, but they're not. They say, "She's had a long life. Good for her." Or, "At least she'll be at peace soon." Right, as if the six months of painful torture that came beforehand can be forgotten just like that.

Best thing to say is: "I'm sorry. Is there anything I can do to help?"

I told my friend what the hospice nurse said and he sort of agreed. He could see how it can be in a person's mind subconsciously or viscerally. Great, so now I had two seeds planted in my brain.

I decided to drive home. She was in bed. She was stable. I could drive home and stay a few days and then come back. She was being well cared for by people who were dedicated and seemed to have a real affection for her. And I had the thought in my head that as much as I felt I needed to be there, there was the possibility she needed time to do what she had to do on her own. Maybe, just maybe, my presence there was keeping her from letting go.

If it happened while I was away, I told myself I wouldn't beat myself up over it.

37. Chinese Wisdom

I returned to Concord on October 13 and took a room at the Days Inn down the road from the nursing home. At this point my mother's breathing was shallow and rapid but still steady. She also started to experience periods of apnea. She would breath rapidly for a few minutes and then stop breathing for 15 or 20 seconds. Her eyes were glazed and chalky and most of the time they were open and listless. On occasion she would close her eyes and keep them that way for a few minutes. She hadn't had anything to eat or anything significant to drink in eleven days. None of the nurses or PCAs could believe her strength.

The staff offered me a room on the second floor with a TV and cable and even its own bathroom. I tried to sleep in it one night but had no luck. They then brought a big, cushy chair into my mother's room and let me sleep there. Believe it or not, it was easier to sleep in the chair next to my dying mother than on the rehabilitation floor in a narrow bed with side rails and therapeutic pillows. I figured, my time was probably coming soon enough, why rush the experience.

I still had the nagging thought that my presence in the room with her was holding her back. Just in case, I did a lot of walking around the first few nights. I walked the halls, visited with the other residents, took the dog for long walks, went out to lunch and dinner, did a little shopping. I tried to keep busy, and I tried to give my mother every opportunity to leave this world without having to do so in front of her oldest son.

On the afternoon of October 17 I went to a late lunch at a Chinese restaurant on the edge of town, almost into Bow. My friend from Henniker turned me on to the place. The food was very good. I sat by myself at the sushi bar and ordered a few pieces of sushi and a small stir fry. I had a little sake. At the end of the meal the waiter handed me my bill and the customary fortune cookie. Please believe me when I tell you this: I opened the fortune cookie and read the fortune and all of a sudden I knew I had to stop worrying about giving my mother her privacy.

The message in the fortune was:

"Nobody should have to go into the dark alone."

38. Tell Your Mother You Love Her

After lunch on the seventeenth I went back to the nursing home with a fresh perspective. I remembered my father and how the night of his passing I had listened to the words of a screenwriter friend in California, who wisely told me to massage his feet and hands. I took her advice and gave him a gentle body massage. He couldn't talk but he communicated his appreciation of my efforts. To this day I'm convinced the massage helped him to relax and let go.

A massage wouldn't help my mother. She was ultra-sensitive to touch. Even the slightest physical pressure would cause her discomfort and pain. Water dropping with the force of gravity would hurt her. It was like this even before she left for residential care. And to this I could add the anxiety and distrust she had of her surroundings. Clearly, a massage or therapeutic rubdown would not help her release. If anything, it would drive her into a living hell.

She was virtually skin and bones, unable to move any part of her body. She probably could not hear or see. So frail, so very frail.

Just before shift change two PCAs and a nurse came into reposition her. These three had known and cared for my mother the past two years. We'll call them F, J, and K. They had grown very fond of my mother. As they were moving her from one side to the other, one of the PCA's was remembering better, brighter days.

"Oh, Judy," she said. "Poor Judy. God, I can remember one time I came into get her up and she gave me such a shot."

They all started laughing, and then they were crying, tears flowing down their cheeks.

J said to me:

"People don't think we get upset because we see it all the time. But we get to know them, you know, and we get to love them, too. It's hard for us when they go. Judy was one of the good ones. She always had a smile." J wiped away her tears. "I'm going to miss her."

After they left I moved into my chair and slid it in close. I rubbed my mother's hair and said things like, "It's OK, Ma. You don't have to be afraid. You're going to a wonderful place. A beautiful place. And you're going to be just fine."

Perhaps this was the night I got that one "look" Patti Davis said Ronald had given to her Nancy. I'm not sure. I'll never be sure. I was rubbing her hair and forehead for a moment, just a moment, her eyes were slightly more clear. She looked at me and opened her mouth to speak. A sound came out. Just a little squeak. It wasn't much. If I were a sentimental man I would say she liberated me from the river of doubt. Unfortunately, I'm not a sentimental man. For all I know she was trying to tell me to leave her the hell alone.

Oh well, remember the fortune cookie, "Nobody should have to go into the dark alone."

Whatever.

Later that night I went for dinner at Longhorn's. I sat at the bar and had a Dewers on the rocks, a double. The bartender was a young woman in her late twenties. My drink arrived and I took a long pull, put my glass down and then stared into it. I could hear the bartender in the background. She was on her cell phone talking to someone about her mother.

She said something about her mother calling and pestering her about stuff, how she talked on and on about her Soaps and her house, and then the bartender went on to say how she had to tell her mother she was busy and needed to go and how she didn't have time to talk about all this mundane crap. When she hung up I asked her if she was close to her mother. She said she was, that they were best friends, but that her mother had been driving her crazy ever since the divorce. "My brother," she said. "That's who I was talking to. He doesn't get it."

I can't remember much else about that night. I have no idea what I ordered for dinner. The only thing I remember is paying the bill, leaving a good tip and writing a note on the check: "Tell your mother you love her."

39. Is it Just a Machine?

I went back to the nursing home with the Dewars still warming my innards. I knew I couldn't massage my mother into the next life. And I knew how super-sensitive she had become to the gentlest of touches. Nevertheless, I had to do something. She couldn't go on like this. She hadn't had anything to eat or drink in thirteen days. Her breathing was short and fast, and her apnea had reached the point where she would hold her breath for as long as forty-five seconds.

One of the nurses had checked her pulse while I was out. When I asked her about it she told me my mother's heart was pumping at 140 beats per minute. I wondered how long it had been beating like that. How many hours? How many days? Could it beat like that for more than a week? Certainly not two weeks. But here we were, going on two weeks.

Crazy and stupid as it sounds, I recalled something I saw in a documentary on indigenous tribes, a medicine man working his hands rapidly over a prostrate body. I don't know exactly what he was trying to accomplish, whether he was trying to heal the person or drive-out evil spirits or both. It didn't matter. I figured, what did I have to lose? I leaned over my mother and played my hands up and down and back and forth over her body, not quite touching her, barely even touching the covers, but moving fast, starting at her head, going all the way down to her feet, then back again and repeating the process. I was trying to generate a field or a vibration. I wanted to draw the last little bit of strength out of her.

I told you. It's crazy, right? The thing is, I had gone back in time to when I was a kid in college. Silva Mind Control was a big hit back then, and a whole bunch of us took an interest in it. We studied the Silva Method as well as other pseudoscientific mental enhancement or empowerment theories.

Silva believed a person could manipulate him-or herself into various states of awareness. In one sleep or pre-sleep exercise (and I'm not sure this was an actual Silva exercise), you would lie flat on your back and imagine waves of energy moving from the bottom of your feet all the way to your head. You had to really imagine these waves. The strength of your imagination had to transcend the intangible. You had to feel these waves. Once you sensed the waves, you needed to speed them up, make them go faster and faster, so that they were oscillating like the vibration in a tuning fork. If you could do this and at the same time fall asleep in the middle of the process, you would find yourself in an altered state of consciousness.

Or so went the theory.[11]

I did this crazy, stupid thing for my mother for about an hour and then I collapsed in the big cushy chair. I watched her for the longest time. Her eyes were open. They were always open. I reached out and closed her lids. They would remain closed for maybe a minute and then they would work their way open again. Other than when she gave me

---

[11] You're wondering if I ever got this to work. The answer is yes, once. It felt like a very, very powerful dream. A dream with physicality and full cognition. Mystics call it astral projection. In my dream I physically moved myself through space to a place I wanted to be. I went somewhere and saw a friend. Did it really happen? Who knows? But I had the best sleep of my life, and the next day, I told my friend about it, and he told me he was exactly where I saw him.

that "look" the previous day, this is the way it had been. For what? Thirty-six hours? Forty-eight hours? Eyes open. Chalky. Seeing nothing. It didn't seem like anyone was in there. It seemed like her soul had already vacated. For God's sakes, I just wanted the machine to stop.

Sleep hit me and I dozed off and on for the next three hours. It felt good to sleep. But every time I awoke and looked out, my mother's unblinking eyes stared back at me. After a while, I stopped closing the lids.

40. Her Last Night

My mother died on a night and at a time when none of her regular nurses and PCAs were on duty. I was there, sitting in my chair, watching her take her last few breaths. It was like an old fashion clock winding down. She didn't gasp. She didn't cough. She didn't have a rattle. She didn't have bouts of apnea. She didn't crunch-up in a fetal position. Her breathing got shorter and faster, shorter and faster, and then . . . she just didn't take in another breath.

Before her last breath, her head was turned toward me and her eyes were open. I looked at her carefully and told her I loved her. I said, "It's OK, Ma, you're going to a better place. You deserve it."

Her jaw moved during that last breath, and part of me wanted to think her soul reentered her body to take one last look at me. It would be of great comfort to think she said goodbye when her mouth moved for the very last time. Too bad for me I'm incapable of that level of sentimentality.

And yet, I am a spiritual person. I find it hard to believe, almost irrational, to think it all ends when the machine we ride around in grinds to a sudden halt. Makes no sense to me whatsoever.

I kissed my mother on the forehead and walked out of the room to get the nurse down the hall. She called the RN from downstairs. The RN pronounced death at 4:30-something. Of course, I was there. I know what time it was. My mom died 4:21 in the morning on October 19, 2011.

I called Sandra, talked briefly and then waited for the funeral director. He seemed surprised when I offered to help him with my mother. He said most people would rather not do it. I was thinking to myself, why? This is the easy part.

We wheeled her down the elevator and through the halls to the car outside. It was a Dodge minivan. My mother would have liked it. As my father always said, she was frugal to a fault.

Epilogue

As a spiritual person I tried to reconcile the painfully slow demise of my mother with my own personal interpretation of what happens at death between body and soul. I mentioned earlier in this diary I wasn't inclined to think of a purely mechanical end to life. But a death by Alzheimer's, or any other degenerative brain disease, makes it difficult to think in metaphysical terms. In a fully functioning adult, when death comes, there is a sense the soul has departed for parts unknown. One moment, the person you know is there, and the next, there is only a nonfunctioning bio-mechanical shell. When my father died, I sensed his presence around me for weeks. In contrast, I sensed no such presence when my mother passed.

A couple of years after my mother's diagnosis, and as her mental capacity deteriorated, I started to rely heavily on the idea that my mother's soul was leaving this world through a metaphysical hourglass, essentially one grain at a time. In my model, a person with the disease would reach a point at which they would have one foot in this world and one foot in the next. The day after, they would be more in the next world than here. And so on and so forth, until nothing remained here at all.

From this perspective, I can jump to an understanding of why I didn't feel the same way when my mother died as when my father passed. His transformation was sudden, compressed. My mother's took years and years.

In my opinion, there is no really good way to die. However, there are truly bad ways. Living in a civilized, modern society, free of violence and far from the ravages of war or conflict, affords us a luxury we often take for granted. It's provincial and naive to view our troubles completely out of this context, because, comparatively speaking, terrible physical and psychological suffering is not that far away. There are places on this earth where men and women continue to inflict horrific pain on one another for little more than their demented pursuit of religious, racial, or national goals. Alzheimer's to a child living in one of these locations would be like a gift from God. Would you choose to live into your eighties and suffer a year or two of myoclonus and contracture at the end of your life? Or would you choose to be raped and tortured or sold into slavery and prostitution at the age of six?

Given this reality, I would not want anyone to come away from this memoir with the idea I am suggesting one terminal illness is worse than another, or that I wish to garner pity for myself, my mother, my brother or anyone else who faces a death by degenerative brain disease. On the contrary, my only wish is to add another voice to the dialogue.

Nobody on this Earth can claim certitude on the subject. Not me. Not Nancy Reagan or Patti Davis. Not the neurologist. Not the research scientist. Not anyone. Nobody can say for sure what's going on in the head of someone who has reached end-stage Alzheimer's. And this leads me to one final comment.

Perhaps it's my bias, but to me, there seems to be a tendency for authors to write a silver lining into their Alzheimer's story, as if they need something (a Deus ex machina) to lessen the horridness of what transpired. I mean no disrespect to Patti Davis or the Reagan family, and I don't mean to single them out in my criticism. It's just that sentimentality and faith about the unknown can, for others, open a door to major disappointment. When we read about a last "look," or find ourselves more affected by the author's emotional personifications than the story itself, I think we do an injustice to the subject matter.

Alzheimer's and its evil brain-robbing cousins are a scourge that rip our loved ones from us piece by piece. In my experience, when the disease is firmly in control, there are no silver linings or wonderfully shared moments.

Our best defense is to plan, way ahead, so that we never have to look back on a missed opportunity or a painful regret.

Bob Bernstein

January 2, 2012

My mother in her new home in Maine, one year before diagnosis. Three years before assisted living.

Left to right. Mom's brother Johnny, who died from a form of dementia, Me, Mom's sister, Mercedes, Mom's niece, Roxanne, Mom's sister-in-law, Bobbie. Five years before assisted living.

Mom at the age of seventeen or
eighteen.

At the resident care facility with G. This was taken about one year after first taking Seroquel. The weight gain is noticeable. One year and four months in assisted living.

My father and me. Waterman Beach Farm, So. Thomaston, Maine. Looking towards the Mussel Ridge Channel.

At the nursing home with end-stage
Alzheimer's.

Judy on her father's lap.
1922.

One week before her death. Finally at peace.

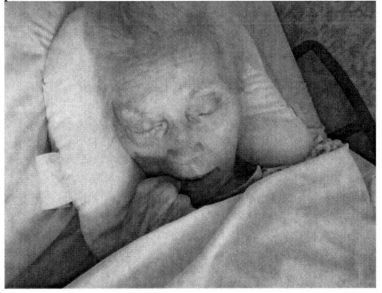

Endnotes

[1]My father had dehydrated because the night before his surgery nobody had started an IV fluid drip. The actual surgery the following morning went very quickly, too quickly, so there had been very little fluid replacement in the operating room. By the time he got to the ICU his kidneys were on the verge of shutting down. From this point on the doctors were playing a game of catch-up.

[2] I love my brother dearly, but he didn't work with my father, nor did he travel with him on business. That "grooming" privilege was given to me, rightly or wrongly, as the older sibling. My father worked with attractive women. He had a personal secretarial pool of four and got phone calls, weekends and nights, from his administrative assistant. He worked for years with the Hollywood elite as a fundraiser in Los Angeles. Jealousy was there, but it was always kept in check. Furthermore, at the time of the surgery, my brother was dealing with dad's doctors, his own very difficult work situation and a serious health issue with one of his kids. I can't blame him for transposing one memory onto another.

[3] I'm not a psychologist or a shrink but it is possible her issue here has its roots in her father's murder. Or as it happens to many of us, she was in denial.

[4] In her words, she would say: "I know how to polish a dime."

[5] Dr. M, a widower for many years, started spending more time with my mom after my father died. He had romantic interests, but they took a back seat to his simply being there and caring for my mother. I was lucky to have him as a thoughtful and attentive companion to my mother. After the

fall, he took her to the hospital and had her checked out. X-rays. CAT scans. Whatever she needed.

6 The list was developed by Thomas Holmes and Richard Rahe, two psychiatrists, at the University of Washington School of Medicine, after studying the records of over 5,000 medical patients.

7 G. was one of the most caring and considerate PCAs at the resident care facility. He worked tirelessly, effortlessly and selflessly. He's a credit to his vocation. There are others, of course, and I will only single them out by their first initials. D. S. A. and J.

8 I can't say enough about the staff at this nursing home. For the most part, they became my mother's end of life family.

9 I'm calling her Doctor E. to avoid using names. For the record, I thought Doctor E. was a very competent doctor; one who made house calls and cared about her patients, which only goes to prove that even the best doctors have severe limitations. In addition, as good as Doctor E. was, her practice and her office's level of care suffered as her patient load increased. I believe this was the result of her turning her patients over to her new PA and resident.

10 From HealingWell.com

11 You're wondering if I ever got this to work. The answer is yes, once. It felt like a very, very powerful dream. A dream with physicality and full cognition. Mystics call it astral projection. In my dream I physically moved myself through space to a place I wanted to be. I went somewhere and saw a friend. Did it really happen? Who knows? But I had the best sleep of my life, and the next day, I told my

friend about it, and he told me he was exactly where I saw him.

Appendix

The Area Agency on Aging for the Capitol Area (AAACAP) Provided the Following Information.

Assisted Living Facilities may be stand-alone facilities, part of a retirement community, or part of a nursing facility. Some may be designed as one room with shared bathrooms (dorm style) or full apartments. Some apartments may be set up with a kitchenette while others may offer full kitchen options. Additionally, they may be residential type settings where an individual has modified a home to accommodate several residents. All Assisted Living Facilities must be licensed if they have 4 or more residents in the facility. What sets an assisted living residence apart from a nursing home is that assisted living does not provide continuous skilled nursing care. The regulations affecting assisted living settings are quite diverse and constantly changing. Basically, most assisted living residences have met local building and fire safety regulations. Some states require special certification or education for key management personnel."
Licensed facilities are designated as "Small" (up to 16 residents) and "Large" (17 + residents), Type A or Type B. There is also a Type C, which are licensed as adult foster day care facilities.

1. In a Type A facility:

The resident must be physically and mentally capable of evacuating the facility unassisted in the event of an emergency. This may include the mobile non-ambulatory, i.e., persons in wheelchairs or electric carts having the capacity to transfer and evacuate themselves in an emergency.

The resident does not require routine attendance during nighttime sleeping hours.

The resident must be capable of following directions under emergency conditions.

The night shift staff in a small facility must be immediately available. In a large facility, the staff must be immediately available and awake.

2. In a Type B facility:

The resident may require staff assistance to evacuate.

The resident may be incapable of following directions under emergency conditions.

The resident may require attendance during nighttime sleeping hours.

The resident may not be permanently bedfast, but may require assistance in transferring to and from a wheelchair.

The night shift staff must be immediately available and awake.

Assisted Living Facilities that have a Certified Alzheimer Unit attached would be licensed as a
Type B. There are some Assisted Living Facilities that have "Memory Units", which are not Certified Alzheimer Units.

3. Certified Alzheimer Facilities

Licensed Type B

Special Disclosure Statement

Activity plan must address cognitive, recreational, and ADLs - specifically

Person designated to plan activities (less than 17 beds)

Must employ activity director 20 hours weekly (17+ beds)

All staff must receive 4 hours of dementia-specific orientation prior to assuming any job responsibilities

Direct care staff must receive 16 hours of on-the-job supervision and training within the first 16 hours of employment

Direct care staff must annually complete 12 hours of in-service education regarding Alzheimer disease.

Type C - Adult Foster Care (AFC) provides 24-hour living arrangement with supervision for persons who, because of physical, mental, or emotional limitations, are unable to continue independent functioning in their own homes. Providers of AFC homes must live in the household and share a common living area with the clients. Services may include minimal help with personal care, activities of daily living, and provision of, or arrangement for, transportation.

Type E - Residents require only medication supervision and general supervision of safety and welfare. Facility may not provide substantial assistance with activities of daily living. Residents must be physically and mentally capable of evacuating the facility unassisted, must not require routine attendance during nighttime sleeping hours, and must be capable of following directions under emergency conditions.

An unlicensed facility of less than four residents, referred to as a Personal Care Home, can be a very fine facility and should be included in your sampling. There is nothing inherently wrong if a facility does not want to be licensed. There are fees, some modification costs, and some governmental oversight involved with being licensed that some owners just may not want to be involved with. These smaller facilities are generally modified residences. Some will be on quiet residential streets, while others may be in the country with a "farm like" atmosphere.

Once again, you will need to spend some time "shopping around". You will want to be sure that the care is good, the facility is safe, and that your needs can be fully met. The homelike setting may offer more privacy, space and dignity than other options.

The pluses of an Assisted Living Facility is the fact that someone is always on duty to provide for the security of the residents. Further, the staff ensures medication is taken at the right time in the right dosage. It a health crisis develops, the facility will follow the same procedures as one would in their own home, i.e., 911 will be called and the resident taken to the hospital. However , those facilities that are part of a Nursing Facility will have more caregivers; available for an emergency due to physical proximity.

Costs for Assisted Living Facilities vary based upon the amenities that are provided. In fact, it may be even more expensive than a Nursing Facility. Be sure to understand what the charges include or do not include. For example, some facilities include medication administration in their rates, and some charge additional fees for this service. Some contracts discuss level of care and others mention additional costs. Review carefully how these are defined, or which services are provided at each level, who determines which level or additional services the resident will receive, when a resident will need to change levels, who is consulted when a change is necessary, and whether the resident can appeal a decision regarding a level change.

[Questions you may want to ask:]

If a resident slips and falls once, does this constitute a "fall hazard" increasing the level of care costs? Does the contract state whether assistance is available around the clock or only during specified hours? Under what conditions may a contract be terminated? Under what conditions are deposits refunded if a resident chooses to leave the facility? Is there an appeal process? Some facilities state that they allow residents to "age in place". What does this entail? How does the facility assist a resident being discharged?

[You should] read the contract closely to be sure everything is clear to you. The contract is a legal, binding document not to be taken lightly. Take it home and read it carefully before signing. Ask for clarification on anything you do not understand. [If you need additional clarification or have doubts] take it to an attorney specializing in Elder Law.

This page marks the end of What They Don't Tell You about Alzheimer's.

CPSIA information can be obtained at www.ICGtesting.com
Printed in the USA
LVOW13s1922161213

365565LV00002B/466/P